D0551191

ROBERT REDFORD

ROBERT REDFORD

David Downing

W. H. ALLEN · LONDON
A Howard & Wyndham Company
1982

Copyright © 1982 by David Downing

Phototypeset by Tradespools Ltd, Frome, Somerset
Printed and bound in Great Britain by
Mackays of Chatham Ltd, Kent
for the Publishers, W. H. Allen & Co. Ltd,
44 Hill Street, London W1X 8LB

ISBN 0 491 02977 2

This book is sold subject to the condition that
it shall not, by way of trade or otherwise,
be lent, re-sold, hired out or otherwise circulated
without the publisher's prior consent in any
form of binding or cover other than that
in which it is published and without a similar
condition including this condition being imposed
upon the subsequent purchaser.

For all the
electric horsemen

Contents

The publishers would like to thank the Kobal Collection, Rex Features and Keystone Press Agency for their help in this book.

The Kobal Collection. Pages, 15, 17, 20–29, 31, 33, 37, 49, 53, 55, 58–59, 60–61, 66–67, 71, 79, 83, 85, 86–87, 90, 94–95, 97, 98–99, 100, 102, 106, 109, 110–111, 114, 116, 117, 120, 122, 123, 124–125, 127, 130, 134, 136–137, 139, 140–141, 143, 144–145, 147, 148, 149, 150, 152, 153, 166–167, 181, 202–203.

Rex Features. Pages, 19, 21, 23, 44–45, 69, 89, 93, 113, 118–119, 161, 162–163, 169, 170–171, 174, 176–177, 179, 182, 184–185, 187, 188–189, 192–193, 195, 197, 205, 207, 213. Also all pictures used in the colour section.

Keystone Press Agency. Pages, 27, 63, 81, 128–129, 132–133, 159, 173, 201, 211.

Beneath a painted sky

CHARLES ROBERT REDFORD, Jnr, the first and only child of Charles and Martha Redford, was born in Los Angeles on 18 August 1937. It was the tail-end of the Great Depression and Charles Snr, like many others, needed two jobs to make

13

ends meet, delivering milk in the morning and working as an accountant in the afternoon and evening. The family of four—Martha had another son by a previous marriage—lived in Santa Monica, some ten miles due south-west of the Hollywood Boulevard.

As Charles Jnr was learning to walk and talk war was spreading around the globe, and the economic wheels began to turn at more like their optimum speed. Better times arrived for America, and for the Redfords. Charles Snr got a good accounting job with Standard Oil of California, and the family was able to move across the Santa Monica Mountains to the better-heeled area of Van Nuys. It was here that Charles Jnr attended high school in the post-war years, displaying a remarkable lack of enthusiasm for formal education. He preferred scaling Hollywood buildings to reading books, and as a result accumulated a long line of bad grades and report cards. Sport was the dominant interest of his peer group, though in the young Redford's case a stubborn artistic streak had already surfaced in a love of sketching.

He had no more complaints of his parents than anyone else growing up in such a place at such a time. 'My mother was a good woman, a joyous person who found the positive in everything. She was full of life. Both my parents were very straight. They believed in sacrificing for the children. They were terrific, very loving.' But they were also 'part of the

Trying to get through. With John Saxon in War Hunt *(1962)*

14

ethic of the fifties', which the young Redford found hard to swallow. 'The fifties
had no personality. As teenagers we had
nothing to identify with. And nothing
originated from the generation I was in.
We didn't project anything of our own. We
just took what was given us secondhand,
changed it a little bit and went on. It was
boring and maddening, and it bothered
me. I wanted out of it.'

It was the era of rebels without causes—
the latter would be supplied in the sixties.
Growing up at this time was to leave its
mark on Redford, just as it was to pro-
foundly influence his future co-star Jane
Fonda. Both were to confront the sixties
explosion as adults, to be affected by it
rather than a part of it. And both, in very
different ways, were to be affected by it
more deeply than many who had been a
part of it.

Back in the mid-fifties, with Korea
barely over and Vietnam only a glint in
the Pentagon's eye, the young Redford
played sports, sketched and unscrewed
light-bulbs from the high towers of Hollywood. In 1955, the death of his mother
shocked him into serious consideration of
the future. Feeling 'less of an obligation to
stick around', he secured a sports scholarship to the University of Colorado. His
time there was to leave two emotions
imprinted on his mind—a distrust of the
American way of sport and a love of the
mountain West. Both would figure promi-
nently in his future work as an actor.

*Searching for a way out of the script! With Michael
Connors in* Situation Hopeless—But Not
Serious *(1965)*

16

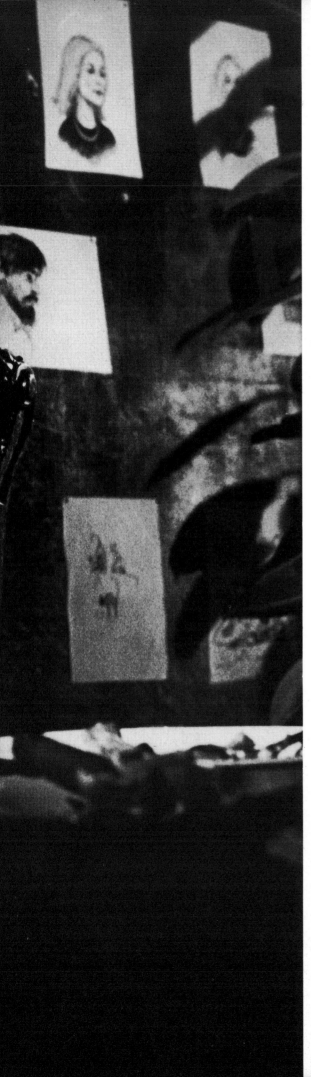

At this stage, though, acting was furthest from his mind. In Los Angeles visits to the cinema had been undertaken as heckling expeditions; only Errol Flynn and Spencer Tracy had escaped his blanket condemnation of the actor as 'sissy'. Hollywood might be sending its magnetic vibes across the nation; the young Redford was close enough to the hype to see through it. 'In those days, you could walk down a boulevard and see the big backdrops at the edge of the studios. And, of course, the backdrop was always a painted sky. There was always this painted sky standing out against the real sky. It impressed upon me vividly that things in movies were unreal. How could I take them seriously?'

At the University of Colorado he was having trouble taking sport lightly. He had chosen the place for its skiing and mountaineering potential, but he was there on a baseball scholarship, which meant endless practice, endless steaks and, presumably, endless locker-room humour. 'One day, suddenly, I realised I was missing something, just going from locker-room to training-room and back. I turned against what that world had to offer me. The competition itself was exciting enough but, once you stepped outside of that arena, there was nothing else. It was another false legacy.'

What was he to do? Cut loose from the educational womb, Redford drifted to and

Opposite: *Waiting for the war to end*
Following page: *The airmen's saviour. Alec Guinness stands in front of the map displaying imaginary German advances*
Both from Situation Hopeless—But Not Serious

19

fro across the States, drinking and sketching with equal enthusiasm. He was enjoying the freedom. For a while he worked in the El Secunda oilfield in California. 'I was a jack-hammer man and I daylighted pipes, which means shovelling oil slick, clearing pipe-lines. I never felt better in my life.'

The money saved from such employment enabled him to make the traditional trip across the Atlantic to Europe, home of high culture. In Paris he led a hand-to-mouth life, sketching on sidewalks in Montmartre, hanging around the American-frequented Harry's Bar until someone bought him a meal. Caught up by his 'hunger for action' in a student demo he was clubbed by policemen 'who didn't know I was just someone from Van Nuys. It didn't radicalise me; it sobered me up.'

These were heady days for Redford, and in later years he would frequently refer back to them as if talking about a lost love. It was 'an atmosphere of no resources, no hopes, no expectations, just an absolutely neutral place to spring from. It was such an open time—your mind was so open, you had no pre-dispositions. I didn't know anything. I didn't know anybody. I just had a lot of energy and wanted to learn. I always learned more from the streets, from meeting people, or from experience, than I did from any books.'

Painting was an important part of his life, and though his canvases tended towards violent gloom, the experience of creating them was a liberating one. It satisfied Redford's intense need to grasp for the individualistic, a need that has remained constant. 'When you are painting', he later said, 'you are absolutely your own man. Nobody comes in and tells you that you can't use the colour red, because the network doesn't like red. The decisions are totally your own, and there is a satisfaction in that, that for me, still tends to outweigh the great moments of satisfaction in acting.' This compulsive urge to be in control would inevitably lead him, one day, out of acting and into directing. It would also play a large part in the creation of the Redford actor-persona—a man who will go to great lengths, even into the wilderness, to preserve his sense of control over his own life. It would not, of course, endear him to the Hollywood hierarchy.

He didn't stay in Paris very long. Hitch-hiking around the old continent he came to rest once more in Florence, where he enrolled at an art school. Here he reached a sort of personal nadir. 'I was living in a very, very small room. I had only one outfit and I wore it constantly. I spent a lot of time alone—I mean, really alone. I went long periods without eating, mostly because I didn't have the money, but I enjoyed the fasting. I was wilfully putting myself into a bleak situation.' His conscious thoughts were beginning to echo his disturbed canvases. His art professor was critical of the work he was producing, and Redford retreated to his room to drink, smoke and let his mind wander down uncomfortable channels. 'It was exciting, but then it got frightening because I felt I was losing control of it. And it certainly wasn't anything I could share with anybody. I didn't feel like any of my friends could understand.'

He quit the art school, sold what paint-

With Natalie Wood in Inside Daisy Clover *(1965)*

22

ings he could, and somehow scrambled together the fare home. But it was not likely to be a triumphant homecoming. For the moment he had learned more about himself than he could happily handle. The future superstar returned to Los Angeles, penniless, his aspirations as an artist badly dented, his future a desperate blank.

24

Drifting onstage

Back in LA he found there was no one who could relate to what he had experienced; old friends from Van Nuys were settling into whatever niche they had found, and had no empathy with Redford's self-discoveries. He retreated into himself once more. 'I was just dying a little each day. Heading right downhill, and almost enjoying it. The worse it got, the more I kind of liked it. I really didn't have the energy to come out of it. I might have gone under in some way.'

But living in the same apartment building was a seventeen-year-old Mormon girl, Lola Van Wegenen. She offered him someone who he could talk to, who could help him make some sense of his experience over the past few years. And they fell in love.

His positive instincts revived, Redford decided to take up the study of art once more, this time at the Pratt Institute in New York. He became interested in scenic design for the theatre, and was advised by a friend that the study of acting would help him with both insights and contacts. Setting aside his youthful scorn of actors, Redford auditioned at the American Academy of Dramatic Arts. He had to perform one comic and one tragic monologue. The former was a disaster, which proved a blessing in disguise. By the time he delivered the latter, Redford was so angry with himself and the proceedings that his performance bubbled over with vehement sincerity. The Admissions Committee gave him an 'A' and made hopeful comparisons with Spencer Tracy. He had, they thought, 'a natural ease of expression, good imagination and flair'.

Redford took to the Academy as he had taken to all other establishments of formal education, like a fish on a hook. Yet he still managed to please his instructors. Responding to the opportunity to express himself—rather than to the opportunity to learn from others—he began to discover in acting some of the creative satisfaction he had previously derived only from painting. It was a good time. Lola was now his wife, and the pair lived on Columbus Avenue, she working in a bank to keep them in food and rent while he finished his schooling.

He landed his first professional part while still a student. In the Broadway production *Tall Story* he dribbled a basketball across the stage and uttered the one line: 'Hey, they're in here.' Even this was enough to get him noticed for 'stage presence', and on leaving the Academy he acquired an agent and, soon enough, another part. The play involved, *The Highest Tree*, concerned a nuclear scientist with little time to live and a lot to get off his conscience. Redford's part was small—six lines of dialogue—but it was one more step up the ladder.

The Highest Tree lasted twenty-one performances, hardly an extended run, and early in 1960 Redford travelled West to work in television. The medium was perhaps less fulfilling, but the roles were meatier, and it was easier to be noticed. *Perry Mason*, *The Deputy*, *Tate*, and other similar long-running dramas, featuring resident stars and weekly guest spots, might rank low on the scale of art, but they got watched, both by millions of ordinary people and by the business's talent scouts. And Redford was conspicuously talented. In one early role, as a sympathetic Nazi lieutenant in a *Playhouse 90* production, he earned high praise from reviewers. The

Hollywood Reporter noted that 'newcomer Robert Redford almost steals the show'. The *New York Times* spoke of his 'exceptional contribution'.

He returned to Broadway in the fall to appear in another play, *Little Moon of Alban*. The role of a fervent Irish Republican was smaller than some of those he had essayed on television, but the critics were again laudatory, one going so far as to criticise the play for killing him off too early. There were problems with the production though. Redford felt he was being over-directed, and had trouble coping with Julie Harris' very different style of acting. 'On the first day,' Redford remembered, 'she came into the rehearsal without a script. She had the part down cold. I like to stay loose and allow things to happen, allow characterisations to grow and relationships to evolve onstage. But her responses were all set in cement. There wasn't any room for any chemical interaction between us.' Such problems were to emerge again and again, whenever Redford had to work with actors or actresses—Barbra Streisand and Dustin Hoffman were to be two future examples—who didn't see the business of acting in such an intuitive way as he did.

Little Moon of Alban lasted one performance less than *The Highest Tree*, and the Redfords, now numbering three—daughter Shauna had been born earlier that year (their first child had died aged two months in 1959)—re-crossed the continent for Bob to undertake more television work and his first feature film. The television shows included *Naked City*, *Route 66* and an *Alfred Hitchcock* mystery; the film was *War Hunt*, a psychological study of a combat platoon in Korea. John Saxon played the central character, an efficient killer whose heroism bordered on the psychopathic and vice versa. Redford played a newcomer to the squad, who couldn't fathom the psychopath-hero and who soon found himself competing with him for the heart and mind of the squad mascot, a nine-year-old Korean orphan-boy.

War Hunt was made by the Sanders brothers—Terry as producer, Denis as director—on a moth-eaten shoestring. It was shot in three weeks in the summer of 1961, with none of those comforts associated with Hollywood movie-making. The actors took turns at making lunches and driving the equipment around. According to Redford 'it didn't seem like a movie. It wasn't at all what I imagined movies would be like'.

Two obvious parallels could be drawn between *War Hunt* and another war movie made the same year, Don Siegel's *Hell Is For Heroes*. Both dealt in grainy detail with the same theme—war as both a cause of, and an arena for, human corruption. And both productions were suffused with stars of the future. *Hell Is For Heroes* featured the up-and-coming Steve McQueen and James Coburn. *War Hunt* had Redford, plus the involvement of two star directors of the future. Francis Ford Coppola was driving a truck, and Sydney Pollack had one of the acting roles. In retrospect the enduring friendship between Redford and Pollack, which was to help them make five films together in the next fifteen years, was probably *War Hunt*'s most important legacy.

Opposite: *Bob and Lola*
Following page: *Victims of hysteria. With Brando in* The Chase *(1966)*

26

But the film itself was not without distinction. The *New York Times* called it 'the most original and haunting war movie for years', and noted that Redford himself was 'excellent'. It should have been the beginning of a swiftly burgeoning film career, but not for the last time Redford had managed to sign himself into a contractual prison, promising three more movies to the Sanders brothers for what Pollack called a 'pittance'. Redford didn't like the material the Sanders had in mind. He pulled out and the lawyers pulled in. There would no more films for three years.

Instead, he returned to the theatre. Sated with heavy drama, Redford asked his agents to find him a comedy role. 'They told me, no, I shouldn't do comedy. That was a whole other ballgame.' But he was not impressed by the arguments. 'Acting is acting. So I pressed them to find me a comedy I could at least read for.'

Sunday in New York was the chosen vehicle. The producer, David Merrick, thought Redford wrong for the part, but agreed to audition him provided that the actor paid his own fare from California. He got the part, his first lead role, and his notices were generally better than the play's. One reviewer warned that he would end up 'a matinee idol if he doesn't watch out'. *Sunday in New York* was reasonably successful, lasting several months and eventually being translated onto the screen. Redford, meanwhile, was back on the west coast doing more television work, appearing in such shows as *The Untouchables*, *Dr Kildare* and *The Virginian*. His performance in one television play, *The Voice of Charlie Pont*, was memorable enough to gain him a nomination for an Emmy Award. His career was certainly taking off now, to the extent that he could

afford to turn down $150,000 for a five-year stint starring in *The Virginian*.

Redford preferred the real West, and success had provided him with the money to begin the land-buying spree in Utah which has hardly abated since. From 1962 to 1963 he was involved in building his own A-frame house in the Wasatch Mountains. When superstardom arrived there would be a ready-made place to leave it behind.

While he was thus involved carving out

30

the wilderness, playwright Neil Simon and
Broadway producer Saint Subber were
meeting in New York to discuss the pre-
sentation of Simon's latest comedy,
Barefoot in the Park. They had already lined
up Elizabeth Ashley for the role of Corie
Bratter, a 'fun-loving New York bride'
who wants to unstuff her stuffy husband.
They had Mike Nichols (later of *Catch-22*
and *Graduate* fame) to direct, and Nichols,
impressed by Redford's playing in *The
Voice of Charlie Pont*, suggested him for the

The Bratters, with apple pie coming out of their ears.
Barefoot in the Park *(1967)*

role of husband Paul. It was to be a fortunate choice, both for the play and for Redford.

Barefoot in the Park proved a bona fide Broadway smash, running for four years. Redford left after eleven months, having established himself as an actor who could take romantic comedy in his stride. It was to be his last performance on stage, a fact which he blamed on the mutation of the commercial New York theatre. To compete with television and the cinema, theatre producers were changing the balance of the romantic-sex comedy, substituting risqué for risk. 'The commercial aspects were drowning the theatre's good qualities,' Redford said later. 'I was looking for something with some literary quality, and there wasn't anything for me in that revolution.'

He had turned his back on the safety of television stardom; now he was rejecting an undoubtedly secure niche in the theatre. But he had served his apprenticeship, proved he could act in either high drama or low comedy with equal facility. The cinema industry would still be there to reap the benefit.

'Will someone tie my laces?' Publicity still for Barefoot in the Park

The legal hassles with the Sanders brothers finally settled in 1964, Redford travelled to Germany to take third billing, behind Alec Guinness and Michael Connors, in *Situation Serious—But Not Hopeless*, a cinematic translation of Robert Shaw's satiric novel *The Hiding Place*. Set in the years straddling the end of the Second World War, the story revolves around two shot-down American airman (Connors and Redford) and the apparently sympathetic German chemist (Guinness) who gives them refuge. Unfortunately for the airmen, the chemist comes to enjoy his role as captor/saviour, and persists in keeping the airman tucked away long after the war has ended. They don't know of the Allied victory, because he feeds them imaginative reports of German victories. Eventually he does release them, without informing them that the war is over, and they have to 'fight' their way into Switzerland through a war movie set.

The book is fun, and the movie sounds, on paper, like a captivating piece of entertainment. Depressingly, and Guinness's performance apart, it proved about as riveting as a cardboard nail. Redford blamed the director, Gottfried Reinhardt— he 'was heavy-handed and had a rather Teutonic sense of comedy timing. ... And what he was doing with the camera seemed static, conventional.' The critics, after having their fair share of fun with the title, essentially agreed, and the film was not given commercial distribution until 1969, when it was hoped that it might cash in on the success of *Butch Cassidy and the Sundance Kid*.

Redford's next film, *Inside Daisy Clover*,

offered more scope for characterisation. Daisy (Natalie Wood) is a Depression-era fifteen-year-old who scrapes a living for herself and her half-mad mother at the amusement pier. She makes a record in an arcade booth and sends it off to movie mogul Raymond Swan (Christopher Plummer), who listens, looks, and hypes her to stardom. She meets, and falls for, screen idol Wade Lewis (Redford), but he abandons her during their first night of wedlock. Daisy later learns that he is a secret homosexual. Beset by this shock and the death of her mother, Daisy's career begins to disintegrate. At the end of the movie, at the ripe old age of seventeen, she is a nobody once more, beaten but decidely unbowed.

Redford was advised by many not to take the part of Wade Lewis, for reasons that are transparently odious. And indeed, he only agreed to play the role as a narcissist, not as a homosexual. 'I'd been around Hollywood long enough to know that there was this whole breed of people who were narcissists. Constantly on the take, never on the give. ... I said to Alan Pakula, the producer, "Gavin Lambert wrote this guy as a homosexual. Now maybe he's got strong feelings, but if that's the way you want to do it, then I'm not interested. I'm interested in playing, if anything, someone who bats ten different ways: children, women, dogs, cats, men, anything that salves his ego. Total narcissism."'

And that's the way he played it. But after the shooting was over, someone in some office decided that the movie wasn't quite sensational enough, and a new scene was shot to show that Wade Lewis was a homosexual. Redford was furious. 'It isn't fair to an actor,' he said, 'to direct him and agree on a concept and play it all the way through and have the film finished and then come round from behind without telling him and put something in that re-interprets the role. ... It was another of those little incidents that made me not very anxious to continue in movies.'

Inside Daisy Clover, even with its last-minute addition, enjoyed little more success than *Situation Hopeless*, though Redford himself was considered worthy of praise by several reviewers. He was beginning to find the life of a movie actor somewhat frustrating. 'I had instincts about the picture I wasn't voicing. I'd think, I question this, but I never raised it because I didn't feel qualified. I was just there as an actor and I was hired and that was that.'

He was next hired to play in Arthur Penn's *The Chase*, a violent parable of contemporary America set in a small southern town. It was variously rumoured that he turned down the central part of Sheriff Calder, eventually played by Brando, and the part of Jake Rogers, filled by James Fox, in favour of playing Bubber Reeves, the escaped convict who unwittingly supplies the spark needed to set the town alight. It was not a large part, and most of the scenes featuring Bubber featured only Bubber, so Redford spent a lot of time running through the foliage in front of second unit cameras while the rest of the cast was shooting the main scenes in the studio.

Redford was not worried about this; he spent a good deal of time hunting and fishing while the others were sweating it out under the studio lights. While waiting to shoot their few scenes together, he and Brando conversed about Red Indians and played at trying to outdraw each other with pocketed flashlights.

35

The final product went on release amidst arguments between director and producers—Penn was excluded from the final editing and complained bitterly that he had been hampered throughout—and a chorus of thumbs-down from the critics, who mostly considered the film too portentous for its own good. Redford shared this criticism; he thought the script 'suffered from the "kitchen sink syndrome"—it tried to do too much'. But it could well be argued that most Hollywood films of this (and most) eras tried to get away with not doing enough, and for all its overblown pretensions, *The Chase* remains one of the best acted, and most gripping, American films of the sixties. Penn, Fonda and Redford would all go to greater fame in the ensuing decade, but none of them would make many films of comparable ambition and stature.

Redford's next project—his fourth in less than two years—was another southern melodrama, *This Property is Condemned*. 'Suggested' by a one-act Tennessee Williams play, the film offered Redford his first 'leading man' role, playing opposite Natalie Wood (a firm friend since *Daisy Clover*), and under the direction of Sydney Pollack (a firm friend since *War Hunt*). It looked promising.

Difficulties soon arose. The southern town earmarked as a location for filming wanted nothing to do with anything 'suggested' by Tennessee Williams. The script, drawn up by *twelve* writers, was an appalling mess. Charles Bronson, with second male billing, wanted his part enlarged. The producer, Ray Stark, was loth to leave Pollack, making only his second movie, to his own devices.

The story centres around Alva Starr (Natalie Wood), a southern belle-cum-flirt. Her mother owns a boarding house for railroad workers, and is doing her best to get Alva married off to middle-aged money. Enter Owen Legate (Redford), the railroad company man, whose mission is to lay off the railroad workers (it is the Great Depression era) who keep the boarding house in business. He also becomes embroiled, rather against his conscious will, with the delicious Alva. With everybody's interests thus set firmly on collision course, the story unfolds in predictable Tennessee Williams style. There's ups and there's downs and it ends in tears.

The reviews were mixed, ranging from 'horrendous soap opera' to 'a handsomely mounted, well acted Depression era drama', but for Redford the time had come to take a break from Hollywood. The post-factum tampering with *Daisy Clover*, the arguments surrounding *The Chase*, the production interference with the filming of *This Property Is Condemned*—was it all worth the trouble? He felt he was becoming a pawn that others were moving around the Hollywood board, and the sensation was an unpleasant one. After he had received good notices for *The Chase* the studio-men started talking to him about 'career momentum'. 'They were saying "you gotta work, kid, you gotta move out here, you gotta do a lot of pictures." Well, I didn't like that. I'm not a rebel, but I'm not gonna be dumped on the assembly line.' It was time for taking stock of where he was and where he wanted to be going.

'But I have to go to work ...' With Jane Fonda in Barefoot in the Park

Retreat

The Redford family, now numbering four with the birth of son Jamie, took off for Spain. They lived quietly in a village near Malaga until discovered by tourists, then moved on to Crete. Redford painted and searched enthusiastically for the parts of Europe which had escaped Americanisation. Hollywood and acting were a world away.

After more than six months of this voluntary exile, however, Redford had to return to the States, having previously committed himself to the role of Paul Bratter in the film version of *Barefoot in the Park*. Gene Saks directed, Jane Fonda played Corie Bratter. It was hardly a film to stretch its two stars' talents, and at this point in their careers both were searching for something more than one of Simon's entertaining, but essentially shallow, forays into urban marriage. Fonda was not to make another film so devoid of social import for a decade. For Redford, who by this time had come to loathe the pristine prudery of Paul Bratter, the making of *Barefoot in the Park* proved no help in charting a future course through the cinematic world. Did he really want to spend his life sacrificing privacy and artistic aspirations for the money made in making such silly films?

For there certainly was money to be made. *Barefoot in the Park* was one of the box office smashes of 1967, and the offers rolled in. 'Career momentum' was there for the taking, but Redford seemed unconcerned. He had already rejected *Who's Afraid of Virginia Woolf* (George Segal making his name in the part); now he turned down *Rosemary's Baby* and forced

Mike Nichols into the recognition that he wouldn't be very convincing as *The Graduate*. He just didn't look like he had problems with women.

This reluctance to grab what was there to be grabbed may have stemmed from indecision or confusion, but it seems more likely that it arose from a mixture of determination and shrewd judgement. He was still determined not to join the assembly line, and only to take those parts in those films which genuinely interested him. And he may have judged that the balance had perceptively shifted—that the industry now needed him as much as he needed them. If so, it was a risky judgement to make. It was to prove correct, but only just.

In any case, he would not return to Los Angeles, where 'even the police are actors'. He would sit and ponder in the Wasatch Mountains, waiting for the right offers to be made, the rights parts to play. He would also set about germinating projects of his own, and it was during this 1966–7 period that *Downhill Racer* first saw the light of day. Paramount agreed to back it, offering Roman Polanski the directorship, but a major spanner was soon thrown into the works. Redford had agreed to do a Western, *Blue*, for Paramount, but on reading, a week before shooting was due to begin, the revised script, he changed his mind. Paramount sued and, not surprisingly, lost interest in *Downhill Racer*.

Through 1967, while legal wheels turned and the world went crazy, Redford sat on his mountain. When the dust had settled, and the right part been found, he would descend once more, ready and able to conquer the seventies.

PART TWO

Tell Them Sundance Is Here

Butch Cassidy and the Sundance Kid
Tell Them Willie Boy Is Here
Jeremiah Johnson

The Western mirror

THE WESTERN GENRE occupies a unique position in cinematic history. To a visitor from the Alpha Centauri Film Institute it would doubtless be astonishing that so much footage has been devoted to one period in the history of one portion of one

Previous page: *Shauna, Bob and Jamie*
Above: *Redford as the Sundance Kid (1969)*

46

country. He, she or it would probably conclude that the events occurring in the American centre-west between 1860 and 1910 had some strange and unfathomable significance to the rest of the human species.

The reasons for this concentration were both simple and self-reinforcing. On the one hand, the period in question, being both violent and long gone, provided a fine arena for straightforward escapist entertainment. The issues seemed clear-cut; men could be men and women could be women, Indians could be killed and horse-thieves hung. Happy endings were easy to find because the whole business exemplified the spread of civilisation, progress in motion. America could re-live its own growing-up, could cling to the roots it wanted to believe it had.

On the other hand, more serious film-makers could use this never-never land, with its firmly rooted cinematic tradition, to comment on precisely those issues which the traditional Western took for granted, on the nature of manhood, on law and freedom, on racial conflict. The failures of America could be traced back to the same roots, to the genocide of the Indian, the taming of the American spirit which accompanied the taming of the frontier, the glorification of individualistic violence personified in the gunfighter/lawman. Since each western town was (for cinematic purposes) perched alone amidst the wilderness it could easily be seen as a microcosm of the whole nation. Within that town there was everything: the good, the bad and the ugly, the old and the young, the rich and the poor, the dream and the nightmare. A hero in that town was a bona fide American hero.

For the Hollywood hopeful there was no

easier way to national stardom than through the moral and physical conquest of such towns. He could create a parallel life, through a succession of movies, acting out a particular set of values and version of heroism in simple dramatic situations set amidst the sagebrush. Thus John Wayne came to stand for an aggressive, macho view of American manhood and the nation's role in the world, Henry Fonda and James Stewart, in their different ways, for a gentler, if equally determined, assault on the problems of living. There were many variations, covering the many stock situations. A Reaganite sheriff, for example, would be strong on crime prevention, but not keen on regulating business practices, especially when the businessmen decided they needed some Indian land.

In the fifties and early sixties the Westerns emerging from Hollywood, both for the cinema and for television, faithfully reflected the states of the nation. There were the aggressive statements of the dream's purity in John Ford's cavalry trilogy, the slightly concerned liberalism of the Anthony Mann–James Stewart tetralogy, the general Cold War complacency of the run-of-the-mill 'oater'. But as the sixties progressed all this changed. The complacency disappeared, the concern grew acute, the dream was examined for its flaws rather than its achievements. America was at war once more, militarily in Vietnam and politically at home, and the Western reflected these conflicts. The Indians became Vietnamese, the law-enforcer found it harder to be both 'good' and effective. Those who had, in the fifties, sought the reasons for America's freedom and prosperity in the dreams of the frontier, now sought the source of disenchantment in the violence of that same frontier.

There was no longer a national consensus, and consequently no longer a mutually agreed version of American heroism. Should the law enforcer automatically be the hero, the law-breaker automatically a villain? Should the hero be headed for wedded bliss or a hundred different beds? How important was the letter of the law, and how justifiable was the treatment of the Indians, both for real and on the screen? Most important of all—was the West a better or a worse place for the influx of civilisation? Formally filmmakers had had it both ways, with the frontiersman sacrificing himself for the civilisation which was rendering him obsolete. After all, he had his heroism to keep him warm. But no longer. With Vietnam filling the television screens such simplistic notions of progress seemed inadequate.

Working out all these contradictions gave the Western a new lease of life, producing a purple patch for the genre in the years 1966–70. Indians as colourful cannon-fodder gave way to a wronged and dignified people in such films as *Hombre* (1966) and *Little Big Man* (1970). Redford's *Tell Them Willie Boy Is Here* was to slot into this category, just as *Butch Cassidy and the Sundance Kid* was to be only one of a series of films, including *Bandolero* and *The Wild Bunch*, re-examining the traditional view of the Western outlaw. Other movies re-examined the figure of the lawman, most notably *Hour of the Gun*, another updating of the OK Corral encounter, and *Death of a Gunfighter*. The Leone 'dollar

The future doesn't look so bright. With Katherine Ross and Paul Newman in Butch Cassidy and the Sundance Kid

48

trilogy' and the magnificent *Once Upon A Time in the West* re-examined, with a soured eye, the whole notion of the civilising of the West.

Each of these films was, regardless of its director's or stars' intentions, as much a comment on modern-day America—on law and order, freedom, the war in Vietnam—as they were vehicles for plain 'entertainment'. Entertainment, like most things, is relative. Redford shot to stardom on the basis of his two Westerns because he embodied some point of view, not necessarily articulated, which Americans found relevant. His persona was the right one at the right time, and being a good actor merely gave him the chance to present it. These two films either said what America wanted to hear, or they didn't say what America wanted to ignore. So superstars are made.

A tale of two outlaws

The casting of *Butch Cassidy and the Sundance Kid* took longer than the shooting, and would have made a star-packed movie in its own right. William Goldman, who according to the publicity blurb had devoted six years to researching the career of these turn-of-the-century outlaws, wrote the parts of Butch and Sundance with, respectively, Jack Lemmon and Paul Newman in mind. But this proved to be only an opening bid in a long game.

Richard Zanuck, the head of Twentieth Century Fox, decided that Lemmon didn't have the box-office clout for the sort of blockbuster he had in mind. He wanted a superstar rather than a super actor, and he got Steve McQueen's tentative agreement to play Butch. It was this McQueen-Newman partnership which was offered to the appointed director, George Roy Hill.

Hill didn't think McQueen right for either role, but he could see Newman making a good Butch. Newman was not easy to convince, but the mere fact that he was prepared to consider the idea, when combined with arguments about billing, caused McQueen to withdraw. Hill then thought of Redford for the Butch role. 'I had read Bob for a part in *Period of Adjustment*, my first film, in 1962. I thought he was a very rugged guy, quite physical, with a great deal of underlying warmth. After seeing him in *Sunday in New York*, I knew he could handle comic situations, and that's exactly what I needed.'

Redford was eager to be in the movie. He agreed to play Butch, but then set about trying to convince Hill that he would be better cast as Sundance. Eventually Hill, Newman and Goldman were all

won over. Everything seemed settled.

But no. Zanuck didn't want Redford, who was 'not an outdoors type'. Zanuck wanted Marlon Brando. He presumably had visions of the two smouldering young men—Brando and Newman—out West together. 'Hombre on the Waterfront' or 'One-eyed Hustlers'. Box Office ticket-dispensers over-heating. How could Redford compete?

Unfortunately for Zanuck, and most fortunately for Redford, Brando had, not for the first time, disappeared off the map used by Hollywood moguls. A two week search proved unsuccessful, and the production team gathered once more in Zanuck's office. Warren Beatty's name was the next out of the hat, but this time round Hill stuck to his guns, insisting that only Redford would satisfy him. Zanuck stuck to Beatty, but finally relented when Goldman and Newman supported Hill in support of Redford. By the skin of his teeth he had the role which was to shoot him to superstardom.

After all this, the film came as something of an anti-climax. *Butch Cassidy and the Sundance Kid* is not the most complex of movies. Butch and the Kid ride back to their outlaw HQ at the Hole in the Wall, where Butch puts down a mutiny with a quick kick in the nether regions and then outlines his master-plan. They will rob a particular train both going and coming back. Since the second hold-up will be unexpected, the train will then be stacked with loot. This plan misfires, first because they use too much dynamite, blowing both train and money to smithereens, and second because they *are* expected. A second train arrives carrying a posse, which proceeds to give endless chase. The two outlaws eventually, and somewhat improbably, elude the pursuit by leaping off a cliff, and decide to go to Bolivia where the old and more successful times may be re-kindleable. For a while they are, but only for a while. The posse arrives from the States, gathers the willing aid of the Bolivian Army, and our heroes are about to be shredded by rifle-fire when the film ends on a frozen frame.

So far, so entertaining. It is the sort of film which (in Britain at least) can be shown on television on Christmas Day afternoons, a family film, full of fun and exciting moments, with nothing included which might offend auntie, spoil the taste of the Christmas pudding, or give rise to any spasms of unnecessary thought or emotion. Even the critics recognised this; Tom Milne noting that 'with all its faults, *Butch Cassidy and the Sundance Kid* is an enormously likeable entertainment which is as likely to be underrated as overrated for its fashionable derivation'. He quotes schoolteacher Etta's (Katherine Ross) impassioned speech—'I'm twenty-six, and I'm single, and I teach school, and that's the bottom of the pit'—as evidence for his assertion that Goldman's script is 'always attempting to define and enlarge on even the least of its characters'.

The other side of the coin was put succinctly by David Thomson in his *Biographical Dictionary of the Cinema*. He accused the film of offering 'a debilitating, modish glamour instead of real character'. It would be convenient to leave *Butch Cassidy* as simple fun, an entertaining two hours, to be avoided if someone wanted something more. But unfortunately 'fun films' also carry values and, being 'fun', tend to get them across to the widest audience. In this respect, *Butch Cassidy* has a lot to answer. There is something vaguely rotten

The lovable outlaws. With Paul Newman in Butch Cassidy and the Sundance Kid

53

at its core; a whiff of hypocrisy wafts out between the smart one-liners.

Paulene Kael also quoted Etta's self-analysis, and added: 'It's clear who's at the bottom of the pit, and it isn't those frontier schoolteachers, whose work was honest.' There is more to this criticism than the puritan ethic; *Butch Cassidy* asks for it in the way the story is set up. The appeal to audience empathy is completely focused on the two outlaws—for two hours the watcher is asked to believe that their lives are the most fulfilling he or she sees on the screen. And why? Because they are 'free', because they never do anything obviously 'evil', because they are the underdogs, because they are the best-looking, and because they have all the best jokes.

But who, really, are these guys who keep saying 'who are those guys?' whenever the posse swims into a half-focused blur? On the surface Butch and Sundance are simply a pair of charming, waggish out-laws, who seem to gather an enormous harvest of enjoyment without actually doing much harm. Not exactly Robin Hoods perhaps, but the railroads and the banks are fair enough game, surely? And they obviously like each other so much; they fit together like . . . brothers? One reviewer thought them a 'sort of cool, straight Western version of the old Crosby-Hope relationship'. Another thought them 'a sexy Laurel and Hardy'. Newman himself was less circumspect: 'It's a love affair between two men. The girl is incidental.'

At a somewhat deeper level, the two are children who happen to have drifted into a world full of adults. And, seen analytically, they are very real children, possessed of both appalling selfishness and delightful innocence. As filmed, however, they come

across as simply innocent. Hill's direction and Goldman's screenplay resolutely refuse to turn the coin over. We are asked to believe—'most of which follows is true' the credits announce—that the general population out West, who work them-selves into the ground to scrape out a living, don't mind if their life-savings are lifted from banks and trains as long as the lifting is sufficiently stylish. The only people who do mind are the posse, and they are effectively dehumanised by the device of shooting them at great distances. Rather than being the representatives of the ordinary people, the members of the posse become a vindictive, soulless machine, whose only task is to spoil the lads' fun. Progress here is just a kill-joy.

54

Hence at the beginning of the film Butch remarks that the new bank isn't nearly as beautiful as the old one. The old one kept getting robbed, comes the reply. Quick as a flash the quip is delivered: 'that's a small price to pay for beauty'. It's a neat line, so long as you don't think about it too much, as long as another neat line comes swiftly on its heels. When you think about a bank's function, particularly in the small communities of the West, as a repository for people's savings, the line loses its neatness, becomes offensively smart. The whole movie's like that.

One obvious parallel is with *Bonnie and Clyde*, made two years before. Here too a contempt for ordinary people punctuated the first half of the film, but there was

With Katherine Ross and Paul Newman in Butch Cassidy and the Sundance Kid

55

always a sense of desperation present, which provided the characters with a moral ambiguity which Butch and Sundance completely lack. And in *Bonnie and Clyde* that ambiguity grows through the film, the wisecracks get sparser, things get real, and the comedy slides into tragedy. In *Butch Cassidy* none of this happens, none of it can happen. The heroes joke their way right through to the tragic end. And when that comes it doesn't *feel* tragic; it just feels like the end of a movie. The characters might be dead, but who were they anyway other than Newman and Redford indulging in a fantasy?

So why did Redford want the part of Sundance so badly? It wasn't much of a role in acting terms, and it wasn't that obvious at the start how big the film was going to be. Clearly the role meant something to Redford on a personal level. George Roy Hill noted that he 'brought a great deal of his own personality to the part', and Redford himself admitted to 'a strange identification with Sundance that I can't put my finger on. There was a time when I was very young that I didn't think it would be so bad to be an outlaw. ... The frontier wouldn't have been a bad place to be in the 1880s. ... You didn't turn your back on too many people, but the atmosphere was free and you carved out of it what you could make of it.'

The implication being that in 1969 you no longer could. Sundance is a schoolboy hero, a fast-with-a-gun loner hero who has neither the time nor the inclination to look into himself. But he is also something more. He is a figure of the past, both anti-establishment and anti-society, because both hunger for the future and he does not. He wants no dilution of the rule that only the fittest *individuals* survive; he resents the notion that his life may be affected by the actions of others.

This role suited Redford because he too was, and is, both conservative and anti-establishment, if rather more thoughtful than Sundance. More important it was suited to the times. The collapse of social action in the late sixties would combine a widespread despair for the future with a distaste for the present. The new hero, the new effective individual, would have to be a man and an attitude rooted in, and longing for, the past.

56

Coop

'Where in your history books is the tale of the genocide basic to this country's birth?'(Buffy Ste Marie)

Tell Them Willie Boy Is Here, which completed principal shooting before *Butch Cassidy* was started, but which was released a few weeks after in 1969, offered a vivid contrast to the other film's vision of the West. Directed by Abraham Polonsky, who had been blacklisted in 1948 and had not directed since, *Willie Boy* projected a relentlessly bleak and fatalistic picture of America past and present.

Willie Boy (Robert Blake), a Paiute Indian who has adapted better than most to the White conquest of the West, returns from his ranching job to the reservation to claim his bride, Lola (Katherine Ross). Her father forbids the marriage, and is killed by Willie Boy in an ensuing confrontation. Willie flees with Lola, who is now his bride by capture according to Paiute law. Sheriff Cooper (Redford) sets out after him reluctantly, accompanied by an eager posse composed of nostalgic veterans of the conquest days.

That night Cooper leaves the posse to act as a bodyguard for the visiting President Taft, and while he is away Willie weakens the posse by shooting its horses and wounding one of its members. This encounter is soon turned by rumour, exaggeration and lies into a nascent Indian uprising. Cooper rejoins the posse and the hunt continues.

Meanwhile Lola, realising that Willie will not escape as long as she is holding him back, attempts to leave him. But he

Previous page: *The sheriff stops for peaches*
Opposite: *An unsatisfactory relationship. With Susan Clark*
Both from Tell Them Willie Boy Is Here *(1969)*

60

finds her hiding place, and she agrees to go on. The next day the posse find her corpse; whether she has died by her own or Willie's hand is never disclosed.

Sheriff Cooper eventually catches up with Willie, now proudly arrayed in his father's ghost shirt, a symbol of his shedding of the white man's world. Cooper kills him in a shoot-out, only to discover that Willie's gun was not loaded. He then allows the Indians to arrange a traditional burial, despite the law's insistence that Willie's body be brought in.

This plot bears some similarities to that of *Butch Cassidy*; in both films the heroes' crimes are to do what comes naturally, and they have to die because the rest of society no longer finds their 'naturalness' an acceptable form of conduct. But there is one crucial difference. Butch and Sundance don't have to be outlaws, a fact which the script does its best to smother in smart jokes, whereas Willie can't escape the consequences of being born an Indian.

Other parallels can be drawn between *Willie Boy* and *The Chase*. In each film one man on the run crystallises social tensions, turning the hunt for him into a violent expression of divided communities. In both films the sheriff seeks to apprehend the criminal because that is what he is paid to do, not because the capture will bring him any personal satisfaction.

But here too there are important differences. Bubber Reeves, the escaped convict in *The Chase*, is given little character; he remains a marginal figure, the film's catalyst rather than its central figure. Willie Boy *is* the centre; he stands for an oppressed people, and his journey towards an inevitable and dignified death is an odyssey of his people's despair. The sheriffs differ accordingly. Brando, in *The Chase*, is the uncorruptible heart of the community, and it is his eventual descent into the community's violence which exemplifies Penn's despair. Redford's sheriff, by contrast, is a pillar without a moral code. He trusts no one, including himself, and his actions are dictated by events, not by personal involvement in the issues at stake. When he makes his gesture to the Indians at the end of the film it is only a gesture. He keeps his badge. He would do it all again.

Some of the critics found *Willie Boy* too despairing. Tom Milne wrote that the characters were 'so pared, the settings so subjugated to the image of bleak despair, that one begins to find oneself seeing them as symbols rather than people'. Paulene Kael also questioned Polonsky's technique, but her basic argument was with the film's overall tone. 'If Americans have always been as ugly and brutal and hypocritical as some of our current movies keep telling us, there's nothing for us to do but commit geno-suicide. That's what *Tell Them Willie Boy Is Here* suggests we should do ... here's a movie that goes all the way—turning white Americans into a race carrying blood guilt, a race whose civilisation must be destroyed.'

This was unfair. The facts of the Indian genocide speak for themselves, and the still-shameful treatment of the survivors' descendants provides at least one good reason for re-stating them. Nor should Polonsky have been criticised for in some small way atoning for Hollywood's own criminal treatment of the Indians (a treatment which is now being reserved for the hapless Mexican). And finally, *Willie Boy* was made in 1968, the climactic year of both the Vietnamese War and the anti-war movement; its relevance as a statement on racial conflict and its resolution

through violence could hardly have been stronger. The film, for all its weaknesses—the casting of Katherine Ross plus boot polish as Lola, the over-didactic tone, the transparently artificial twisting of the plot to score political points, the over-simplification of the Indian characters and Indian life—made a powerful cinematic statement, a fact which could only be emphasised by the near-simultaneous release of the slick and empty *Butch Cassidy*.

Redford himself found much to argue

with in the film, and his liking for the finished product seems to have diminished with time. Initially he could say: 'I liked the movie. I liked what it was trying to say.' But later he would include it in his list of 'mucked-up projects'.

He enjoyed working with Polonsky. 'I had an enormous liking for him. All I could think of was this man who'd been in a time capsule falsely for twenty-five years. He came out with a kind of energy that was irresistible. I felt very compassionate

Bob, Lola and Shauna

about that.' But Redford was most unhappy about the casting of two non-Indians to play the two main Indian roles. 'I was sick of seeing Indians—many of whom I had known personally and been friendly with—depicted on the screen in a way that really annoyed me. And I thought what better opportunity than this, a real Indian story, to let the Indians play themselves.' The studio, though, wanted to use their contract players. 'Their priorities are always goofed up,' Redford commented, 'they just think of using up people instead of looking at the potential of the characters as they are written or as they could be played.'

Redford didn't agree with the way the Indians were portrayed either. 'I felt the Indians were essentially a people of behaviour and sign language, that it was a mistake to take what I thought was a thirties protest platform and put it in the mouths of an alien cultural group.'

But he did approve of his own character, Sheriff Cooper, 'because of the man's neutral position to what was going on. It was in the grey area that I am rather fond of in films. He saw the good and bad on both sides. . . .' This was one of Redford's more revealing statements. Sheriff Cooper, far more than Sundance, epitomises the Redford hero-persona, the one which was to prove so acceptable and so lucrative in the seventies. This figure has most of the attributes of the old hero—including the Gary Cooper figure whose name he shared—such as good looks, effectiveness in combat, and an apparently functioning conscience. The main difference lies in the degree of moral certitude. The old hero always knew, deep-down, why he was standing up to be counted, what he was being effective for, and so acquired a

certain nobility. Sheriff Cooper has too many doubts to be noble; he cannot rise above the conflict because he carries it around within himself. He is still effective, but he would also be pathetic were it not for the fact that he is aware of his weaknesses and doubts. His lack of pretence or self-deception is what gives him heroic stature. Where an Eastwood or a Bronson would cut through the doubt by instigating action, the Redford figure simply accepts that there is no way out. It's all grey and he's as confused about it all as you or I. He chooses only when he has to, without the support of a moral code to choose by.

Previous page: Redford receives an Oscar as Best
Director for *Ordinary People*
Opposite: With Will Geer in *Jeremiah Johnson*
Above: With Paul Newman in *The Sting*
Below: A scene from *All The President's Men*

Following pages. Left: With Barbra Streisand in
The Way We Were. Right: A Bridge Too Far

Above: A scene from *All The President's Men*
Below: With Faye Dunaway in *Three Days of the Condor*
Opposite: The Electric Horseman

Following page: Brubaker

'With our future rush, our need to expand and grow at any cost, we have lost something. Something vital. Something of passion and romance. But, perversely, I find that as technology advances us into the future with stunning innovations, I become more interested in the past.' So Redford wrote in his book *The Outlaw Trail*. In his third Western, made some three years after the first two, he was to play a character in search of that which was 'lost'.

The script for 'Liver Eatin' Johnson', later refined into *Jeremiah Johnson*, was a splicing together of two books: *Mountain Man* by Vardis Fisher and *Crow Killer* by Raymond W. Thorp and Robert Bunker. Both had been exhaustively researched rather than simply cobbled together; Thorp and Bunker had obtained detailed material about Indian life in the relevant space-time slot from the Bureau of American Entology. 'Liver Eatin' Johnson' was nothing if not authentic. Still, so, for that matter, is a cow-pat.

Redford showed the script to director friend Sydney Pollack, as a potential candidate for the joint venture they had both been watching out for. Though somewhat turned off by the liver consumption, Pollack liked it, especially the first fifty pages, 'one of the best beginnings I ever read'. It had all the right ingredients—a larger-than-life hero, spectacular settings, enough action, and an overall theme of considerable contemporary relevance. From Redford's point of view the figure of Johnson must have been a sympathetic one, and the acting challenge implicit in a film so short on dialogue must have intri-

65

gued him. But any well-written script which managed to encompass Utah, the Indians and the natural heritage of the West would probably have had his backing.

The studio bosses were something else altogether. They tended to want more than mountains, the odd nod towards conservation and no dialogue. Redford in the starring role was an obvious plus, but Warner Brothers was still less than anxious to sink a fortune in someone else's idea. Redford had already received his advance when someone panicked over the budget, and threw the whole project into jeopardy by ordering Pollack to shoot the entire movie on the company back lot. This, though large, included few mountains. Pollack considered pulling out of the project, but Redford had already spent his advance. Eventually a compromise was reached whereby the film was shot on location for the same sum of money which it would have cost to shoot it on the back lot. Luxuries like dressing rooms, wardrobe designers and such were dispensed with. And to make matters worse, the weather refused to cooperate with the schedule.

The film was set in the first third of the nineteenth century, considerably earlier than most Westerns. Jeremiah Johnson arrives from the East, determined to abandon civilisation for the freer life of the mountains. The film follows him on a trek of discovery, as he finds out that nature, like civilisation, has a code which cannot be ignored or escaped. He almost perishes in his first year 'out', but is saved by a chance meeting with an older, more experienced hand (Will Geer), who sets about teaching him the tricks of the survival trade. Once educated in the new code, Jeremiah goes off alone again, through a string of further encounters. These provide him with a 'wife' (given to him by the Flathead Indians) and a mute 'son' (whose father has been killed and mother driven crazy). At the turning-point of the film these three are settling into a largely non-verbal life together.

The first half of *Jeremiah Johnson*, rich—some said over-rich—in Indian lore, has all the charm and drama of a Jack London story. It is what Redford calls 'how-to' cinema; the audience is being instructed while it is being entertained. Johnson is a heroic figure because he chooses to risk his life in an alien environment, chooses the life of the Indian, unprotected from the rigours of nature by civilisation's walls. His effectiveness does not rest on other people's ineffectiveness.

Then came the problem. How to turn this successful escapee from corruption into a berzerk killer of Indians? Pollack and Redford agonised over their dilemma. 'We can't kill all those Indians,' Redford said; 'how can we make a picture killing all those Indians?' But killed they had to be; Jack London stories are not commercial cinema. 'I know it, I know it,' Pollack replied. 'But what are we going to do. I mean, we've got to get it so that when the Indians kill your family it's not their fault. You've gotta screw up, you know?'

In other words, the mountain man had to be joined to the crow killer using invisible stitching. The answer, thought up by some bright spark in the team, was

Previous page: *Jeremiah arrives from the East*
Opposite: *The killer of indians*
Both from Jeremiah Johnson *(1972)*

68

for Johnson to agree, reluctantly, to guide a US cavalry mercy mission through an Indian burial ground. The Crows had their reason for killing his family, and he had his reason for killing Crows. Neat, eh? It was a device which worked both philosophically and box-office-ly. As Patricia Erens wrote: 'the crossing of the Crow cemetery symbolises the unavoidable consequences of human action. There are no right or wrong decisions—no good and bad sides—there are only choices.' And, by some strange quirk of fate, this particular choice turned the second half of the movie into a succession of violent encounters between the revenge-hungry hero and a long queue of Crows. Nanook of the West mutated into the mountain version of *Death Wish*.

The critics were divided. Judith Crist wrote: 'Pollack's achievement is his sustenance of the mood of heroic legend; Redford's is that he becomes as large as the heroes thereof—and as eternal. Yield—and you will encounter a film of penetrating beauty, and an experience that you will inevitably assimilate.' Paulene Kael didn't feel like yielding. She thought the whole film was rigged to supply both fresh fodder to the liberal conscience and a level of violence sufficient to appease the bloodlust of audiences weaned on *The Wild Bunch* and *Dirty Harry*. She concluded that the film seemed to have been written 'by vultures'. Far from seeing Redford as eternal, she compared him to Lassie— 'sheepish, silent and straight'.

Both points of view seem valid. Either way, *Jeremiah Johnson* is one of the few memorable Westerns made in the seventies, original in both its choice of time-setting and the characterisation of its hero. Johnson, unlike Shane or Wyatt Earp, was not bringing civilisation to the West, not clearing ground, raising crops or animals, erecting fences or laws. He was fleeing from all that. For him in the 1830s, as for many in the 1970s, the future threatened more than it promised. And then, as now, it was possible, if hard, to rediscover the natural immediacy of life. All it took was courage and willingness to learn.

This basic thrust of the film was certainly weakened by its midstream transition into a traditional no-holds-barred Western. But perhaps an hour of violent battle is the lowest price commercial cinema can pay for bringing an hour of 'Jack London' to the silver screen. It might be a shame, but vultures will be vultures, at least most of the time. Redford himself was satisfied. 'I loved *Jeremiah Johnson*. I loved doing it, and I loved the overall film.'

The western survivor. Jeremiah Johnson

70

A hero for the seventies?

These three Westerns offered a picture of the Redford hero-persona which, for all the differences between the three characters, was surprisingly consistent. There was, of course, the good looks, the blue eyes, the golden mop, the flashing teeth. Redford was a sex object, sure enough, but he was not coming over in an aggressive, macho manner; there was no need for male audiences to feel competitive. On the contrary, his role in *Butch Cassidy*, as partner and buddy to Butch, so overwhelmed his relationship with Etta that men could wallow in the male camaraderie.

There was nothing new or special in this. Handsome buddy-buddy characters were as old as the hills they rode. Similarly, Redford's characters' coolness, resourcefulness and willingness to kill (when it was absolutely necessary) had marked many a Western hero, through James Stewart, Henry Fonda and Gary Cooper.

It was the differences which were crucial. The events of the late sixties had eroded the hero's certainty, and had established an anti-establishment posture as necessary to the hero's credentials. But here he ran into the same difficulty as the society which created him. The sixties had raised expectations which could not be fulfilled; they had exposed the 'lie' without offering a sustainable new 'truth'. The new hero had to be anti-establishment, alright, but what was he *for*? There was no newly acceptable code for which he could stand.

One way out of this dilemma was that chosen by the Eastwood/Bronson persona. Their new hero would be the individualist who supported the traditional values against an establishment which had forsaken them. He would make the past work in the present. This was doubly convenient in that it allowed him to take on both the criminal and the established powers, the former allowing full rein to his violent effectiveness, the latter establishing his contemporary credentials. It was the Lone Ranger brought up to date; now both the villains and the sheriffs had reason to dread his hi-yo silvers.

The problem with this approach was that it sailed pretty close to fascist cinema. It brought the values of the frontier to the city (most explicitly in *Coogan's Bluff* and *Death Wish*), and so offered a fantasy solution to real difficulties—one violent maniac willing and able to defy everyone and everything. All the films were rigged to make this seem reasonable, but the very visibility of the rigging was cause for more than concern.

The Redford persona has occasionally slipped into this sort of heroism. Both *Butch Cassidy* and *Jeremiah Johnson* come close, but the former film is saved by its warm and superficial tone, the latter by its authenticity. Redford, in any case, is not made for such a heroic persona; he is too thoughtful and too concerned with the world outside the cinema to fit comfortably in such roles. His archetypal hero-figure cannot take the easy way out, and although he has to remain effective in combat—all cinema heroes do—he cannot create a code around that effectiveness. He is basically a confused hero, a true seventies figure. Though certain of his own effectiveness, he's far from certain of how or why or when it should be used. Rather than bring the past into being to set the present right, he would prefer to drag the present back into the past, back to a time when the land was free and simple,

camaraderie was enough, and one man really could decide his own life, before it all got so damned complicated. Because he knows it *is* complicated. Sundance is what he'd like to be, but Sheriff Cooper is what he is, someone torn between what's probably right and what indubitably is, someone who can't fool himself into believing that the two can be easily reconciled. He's the one who keeps going even though there's no answers. His heroism lies in his moral survival.

PART THREE

'America the Beautiful'

Downhill Racer
Little Fauss and Big Halsy
The Candidate
The Hot Rock
The Sting
The Great Waldo Pepper
Three Days of the Condor
The Way We Were
The Great Gatsby

Golden boy

THE ENORMOUS SUCCESS of *Butch Cassidy and the Sundance Kid* turned Redford into an 'instant' superstar. With all the assurance of long practice the media machine wiped off his eight years of screen appearances and proclaimed him an overnight sen-

77

sation. It was real because the machine said it was real. Redford would 'walk down the street and see my face staring out at me from newsstand after newsstand and I just wanted to go someplace and hide'.

Success didn't alter his view of the Hollywood establishment. In an interview early in 1970 he noted that 'the film industry is jostling with $50,000 a year men, anxious, talentless. They ought to have been lopped off the tree years ago. But they cling to it like limbless wonders. You have to fight them.' Their basic approach was not conducive to the making of good films. 'You can't run an art form like a business anymore, and they're still trying to. Films to them are just like vacuum cleaners or refrigerators. The approach sickens me.'

Redford wasn't about to swallow the studio's publicity on his behalf. 'When all that crap about golden boy, big property, wow-at-the-box-office is blurbed, I take off. I did before. I'll do it again. No one makes a commodity out of me.' He took his success, like his acting, pragmatically. He could always leave the hype-polluted Hollywood air for the clean winds of Utah.

There he could attempt to hang on to the tattered threads of his anonymity. Redford wasn't going to sacrifice his private life, wasn't going to expose his innermost feelings and thoughts or the life of his family to the carrion crows of the media machine. Nor did he see any reason why he should. 'The idea that an actor owes the public something is a constant running battle I have with publicists and people at studios and even friends and fellow actors who don't share my opinion. I've always believed that I owe a performance and a contribution and that's it. I have no obligation to appear publicly for anything I don't want to. I have no obligation to share my private life with the public.'

Predictably enough, Redford's withdrawal from the slings and arrows of outrageous success only served to confirm and strengthen his personal views on the road to self-fulfilment. He was a loner by instinct, and now circumstances were forcing him to be a loner by necessity. Utah was not only beautiful, wild and free, it was also a much-needed haven. He believed a man should go his own way, carve out his own life in the best way he saw fit. Now he could afford to do just that. Now he had little choice but to do just that.

Going to Hollywood, he thought, was 'a little like making a mission behind enemy lines. You parachute in, set up the explosion, and then fly out before it goes off.' The suspicion was growing that, to Redford, Hollywood was becoming synonymous with modern society in general. He preferred the past to the future, and probably to the present as well. 'We have a technological advancement today,' he said in 1972, 'but it's very sterile and it doesn't seem to include much room for human behaviour, emotion or life. There's been little consideration of what animal, plant and human life is going to be like in the future—it's all how machines, computers, are going to operate. That's not exciting to me and never has been. ... Perhaps I'm a romantic without illusions, whereas in the past they were romantic and full of illusions. To me it's better to live by your own wit and instincts than to be geared to

As David Chappellet. Downhill Racer *(1969)*

a computerised existence. ... I'm interested in the individual's fight to be himself.'

And particularly in the superstar-actor's fight to be himself. Redford had always harboured an ambivalent attitude towards his profession, and towards his own involvement in it. He was constantly sinking himself into alien characters—no matter how close they came to his self-image they remained alien—and his admirers were constantly mistaking him both for the characters and for figments of their own imaginations. He insisted on seeing acting as just a job, but clearly it was a job with a difference, and one which both suited and repelled him. In an interview in the mid-sixties he tried to explain his feelings: 'Ego plays a very important part in it, no matter what anybody else says. I don't believe those people who say they're in acting just for the truth of it. I would tend to believe someone more who said, "I am just in it for the money." I would believe that. And who said, "I want to be a star, and I want people to love and adore me." I would believe that. And I would admire and respect somebody who said that! Not somebody who said, "Gee, I don't know why I am an actor. I don't want to be seen, I don't want people to be interested in me...." I can't believe, putting yourself up, subjecting yourself to exposure in front of hundreds and sometimes millions of people doesn't involve ego. It sure does in my case.'

And yet Redford didn't like his face plastered across the known world, didn't enjoy the parasitical attentions of the press, didn't relish the determination of fans who trekked through the wilderness just to catch a sight of the Redfords at breakfast on their porch. It was not just a matter of wanting to have his cake and to eat it; it was a matter of preserving the balance within his own head, of keeping the unreality of stardom at a manageable level, of paying a certain price for a certain reward. To do what he wanted to do, both within and without the world of cinema, he had to accept some and deny some of the 'rules' governing a star's existence.

Paradoxically, the retreat to Utah preserved both Redford's internal balance and the superstardom which had threatened it. He became a latter-day Garbo-figure, and his mountainous version of her 'I want to be alone' encouraged rather than dissipated public interest. It fed the myth, and provided him with that aura of Olympian detachment which was so large a part of his appeal to the disillusioned seventies.

He was not yet, of course, as big as he was going to be. *Butch Cassidy* had shot him into orbit, but he still had to stay there. He had enough clout now to push his own projects, but not enough to get them accepted if they strayed too far beyond the studio's definition of commerciality. He had little money of his own—he was still working off the Paramount contract, making films for less than his current status would have suggested, and all this income was being taken up by the expansion of his mountain retreat. His name was now akin to a credit card; the limit was high, but it was still a limit. It had to be cashed again and again. If he wanted more artistic freedom, Redford was going to

Redford and his family strolling along New York's Fifth Avenue, July 1971

have to make films dear to the company's
heart, as well as those dear to his own. The
next five years would produce such a
mixed bag.

Winner or loser. Downhill Racer

Enjoying breakfast with the family

Winners are losers too

For Redford, success was more than just an experience; it was also a matter for frequent reconsideration. He had now encountered the American success ethic at work in both sports and the film industry. Perhaps more important he had been born into success, not particularly in a family sense, but into a nation which was inheriting world dominion as he grew up. In the fifties the suburban dream was still basically pure, untainted by the cynicism of

83

later years. The world of the thirties and forties, of failure and war, had give birth to a new dawn. In such a world everyone could be a winner, and everyone should be a winner.

Redford did not knock success *per se*. 'American society,' he recognised, 'is structured in such a way that you almost have to worry about things like that. There is such an emphasis on success you can't not think about it.' To ignore it, in the film industry for example, would be suicidal. You 'might find yourself without the ability to make the next picture you want to make'.

But Redford was concerned about the implications of building a society around such an ethic. 'The truth is that there is insecurity in both winning and losing when you boil it down as we have in America, in politics, in most of the topics that govern our lives. You begin to fear not winning. You begin to fear not getting ahead, and that bothers me enormously.' This judgement was obviously made with his own success partly in mind. 'I think a winner doesn't have it as easy as a lot of people think. He is hit with a combination of the awe and hostility of those people who say: "who are you to be there? what kind of lucky break did you have?"'

In 1969–72, interwoven with the three Westerns already discussed, Redford made three movies which centred around this question of winning and losing. One of them, *Little Fauss and Big Halsy*, was largely a studio attempt to cash in on the *Easy Rider* syndrome, but the other two, *Downhill Racer* and *The Candidate*, were projects which Redford himself chose to push. All three films projected variations on the same basic theme, that the monomaniacal pursuit of success is essentially self-des-tructive, and that any victory gained in such a manner is necessarily pyrrhic. None of Redford's characters in these films is sympathetic for very long; what charm they do possess is swept away by the determination to win.

Downhill Racer was seen by Redford as an examination of the success ethic at work in American sport, and as such was considerably tempered by his own experience of the athlete's life. The genesis of the film occurred in pre-*Barefoot in the Park* days; it was then that Redford asked James Salter to construct a script around an American skier's attempt to strike Olympic gold in the downhill racing event. Paramount was interested, but then came the *Blue* fiasco, and the company's suing of Redford. The provisionally appointed director, Roman Polanski, was also way behind his shooting schedule for *Rosemary's Baby* (also for Paramount), so the company was in no mood to press ahead. It rejected Salter's script and the whole idea was back to stage one.

This proved a blessing in disguise. According to Redford, Paramount was not really interested, in fact didn't even understand, what he wanted to do. 'It wasn't supposed to be a picture about skiing, although the studio never got that through their heads.... I wanted this movie to be the portrait of an athlete, of a certain kind of person in American society.... It annoyed me the way athletes were portrayed in films. They were always clean-cut, middle-American types who came off the

Opposite: Downhill Racer
Following page: *Après ski with Camilla Sparv, also from* Downhill Racer

84

farms and had great wives behind them and great moms and dads. It was a Norman Rockwell depiction of America and that's not the way I saw it. I said "what about the athlete who's a creep?" We do tend to tolerate creeps who win. Who remembers who came in second? I wanted to see that in a film and it only happened to be skiing because I was into it at that time and thought it was something very beautiful and visual that hadn't been dealt with in film before.'

After the *Blue* hassles had been sorted out, Paramount renewed its interest, deferring to Redford's vision of the film on condition that he used the title 'The Downhill Racer'. On this provisional say-so, Redford organised a team of cameramen and 'ski-bums' to film the 1968 Winter Olympics at Grenoble. There was only one problem—the French authorities were refusing anyone permission to film the races. Redford was not to be deterred so easily. 'We had to use disguises to get by the guards. The photographer was pretty well-known, so I fixed him up with a hairpiece and a false nose so he could get on the slopes with his camera. He loved it. The ski-bums shot a lot of footage too, but they couldn't get by the officials, so they swiped a sign from the refreshment vendor, put it in their car window, and got through that way. Every night we met at our room to see who was still alive. But we came back with 20,000 feet of film.'

Back in America, Redford asked Michael Ritchie to direct the movie. Ritchie

At a press conference

88

had not made a film for cinema before, but his television work had impressed Redford, and the two men soon found that they shared the same vision of the final product. In Ritchie's words, they wanted *Downhill Racer* to be 'as gutsy, as realistic, as harsh and as documentary as possible . . .'. This was not going to be one more Hollywood-style story of man's triumph over his fellows in the sporting arena.

One problem was how to interweave the dramatic plot and the documentary footage of the skiing without losing either the real story-line or the realism of the action. Ritchie achieved a near-seamless join through the use of rapid-fire editing, and through a sustained disregard of precise lighting or camera angles in filming the non-action sequences. It all looked real, and it all looked honest. More important still, within the limits of mainstream cinema, it *was* real and honest.

The plot follows an American country-boy through three seasons of competition and two summer training stints in pursuit of the Olympic gold medal. It is not a 'will he or won't he win' film; he does win as it happens, but this victory is over-shadowed both by the manner of its achievement (a mixture of talent, luck and cold-heartedness) and its obviously transient nature. As he wins, Redford's David Chappellet has his moment of glory dimmed by the brilliant performance of a newcomer; it is obvious that the celebrations will not last for long. His unimpressed father puts it in a nutshell: 'Champions—the world's full of them.'

A secondary theme, which was to loom larger in Redford and Ritchie's *The Candidate*, and which clearly came close to Redford's heart, was the role of the media as distorter of the success ethic. In *Down-*

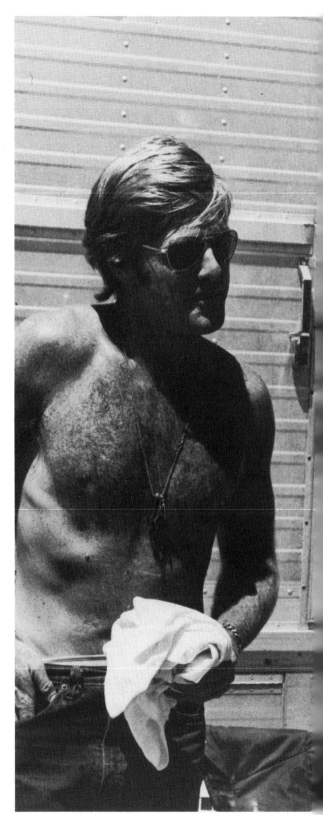

On the set of Little Fauss and Big Halsy

hill Racer the journalists are not interested in Chappellet as either a person or an athlete; he has news-value only as a potential winner. A vicious circle is at work here—the winners alone get the glory, but only because the media ensures that they alone get noticed. Chappellet may be a glory-hungry bastard by nature, but even if he wasn't, the exigencies of survival at the highest levels would turn him into one. It is not his fault that competing now only makes sense in terms of winning, that coming second means about as much as coming nowhere.

As Chappellet, Redford moves from arrogant contender to pyrrhic victor with some of the sparsest dialogue on record. It is all there in the lift of an eyebrow, the rueful expression, the infinitesimal movement of the facial muscles. In some of his films this style of understatement has come perilously close to a lack of statement, but in *Downhill Racer* the balance is perfect. The character is understandable without being sympathetic; his search for glory is both enobled by the sound and fury of the skiing sequences and rendered pathetic by its dehumanising repercussions away from the slopes. As a film about sport and the sportsperson *Downhill Racer* had rarely been bettered.

The critics were generally kind, but the public proved disinclined to disprove the old adage that sporting films were death at the box-office. In subsequent years the film was to acquire something of the respect it deserved. Redford was certainly far from repentant. 'It took two years of my life, but it wasn't very successful commercially. Really the films I've wanted to make and have really been behind haven't made much money. That's the way it is. But you end up with the satisfaction of doing something on film that you have a kind of passion for.'

In *Little Fauss and Big Halsy* the racing was to be done on motorbikes (nearly all of them Yamahas for some reason) at a less exalted level, as the media-infested Olympic ski-slopes were abandoned for the dusty dirt-tracks of the American southwest. The film's screenplay had been written by Charles Eastman, and was, by all accounts, an impressively original piece of writing. Redford thought it 'the best screenplay of any film I've ever done. . . . It was without doubt, the most interesting, the funniest, the saddest, the most real. . . .' Director Sidney J. Furie thought it had some 'wonderful scenes' and 'the best dialogue I ever read'.

So how did this proto-masterpiece turn into such a turkey? Most of the damage was done before a single scene was shot. Eastman wanted to direct his own screenplay, but the producer, Albert Ruddy, refused him the privilege. Eastman, whether out of pique or driven by some nobler cause, refused to help Furie, Ruddy's choice for director. Ruddy, whether out of guilt or driven by some nobler cause, refused Furie permission to tamper with the script. According to Redford, Furie never got the point of Eastman's script. The denouement was predictable. Furie, prevented from making his own film, simply mismade Eastman's.

In addition, Redford himself was preoccupied with *Downhill Racer* business throughout the shooting of *Little Fauss and*

Opposite: *Man and image*
Following page: *Offset with Natalie Wood*
Both from The Candidate *(1972)*

Mc Kay
the better way

Big Halsy, had problems relating to co-star Michael J. Pollard, and couldn't agree with Furie's handling of the story. All in all, it was a mess. Some of Eastman's dialogue survived to shine through, but the film's parts never made a coherent whole.

The story-line followed the two title-characters, played by Pollard and Redford respectively, around the dirt-tracks in pursuit of an ever-illusive entry into the big-time. Fauss is a little runt over-protected by his parents (strong echoes of C. W. Moss in *Bonnie and Clyde*), who initially finds in Halsy a model for emulation and a route of escape. Halsy himself is a twisted composite of Redford characters. He is a Sundance who never met a Butch, a cool exterior without the inner warmth. He is a low-life David Chappellet, whose arrogance is a mask for insecurity, not the expression of an in-built sense of his own talent. Halsy swaggers his way through life, hiding his loneliness and a sense of personal worthlessness. Unlike Chappellet or the 'Candidate' he never even smells success, let alone grasps its thorny branch; he just chases after it, hurting himself and anyone else who happens to get close to him. Fauss does get close enough to learn some of Halsy's ruthlessness, and ends up paying his 'teacher' the supreme compliment—he leaves him in the lurch. Rita (Lauren Hutton), who gets pregnant by Halsy, has the sense to leave him, period.

The moral thrust of the film is somewhat confused. Both Fauss and Halsy are inveterate losers, and the last scene of Fauss speeding past a broken-down Halsy merely suggests that tortoises lose less often than hares. As a chronicle of its times, the film faithfully reflected an America morally at sea, without ever offering any insights into how it had got there or how it might get out. As a comment on the timeless vagaries of the human condition, with Fauss and Halsy as doomed Sisyphean figures, rolling round dirt-tracks rather than rolling rocks up slopes, the film was and is equally vague. Like its racing sequences, *Little Fauss and Big Halsy* seems full of swirling, incoherent noise and dust.

Despite all the problems, Redford enjoyed playing Halsy. Unlike the skier or the politician he had little dramatic depth, and that in itself was a welcome change. 'It was a very different role from what I'd been doing. He's very verbose for a next to illiterate type of guy. He's a rake, an absolute cad, scroungy and raunchy. There was nothing subtle in that role. It was fun to go that way for a shot.'

But only for a shot. *The Candidate*, like *Downhill Racer*, was a Redford-inspired project from the beginning. He originally conceived the idea of doing a film about the American democratic process—politics, like sport, had long been considered a box office no-go area—while watching the 1968 Presidential campaign on television. 'What I saw frightened me. It was so staged. Nixon's telethon looked like it was being broadcast from Madame Tussaud's wax museum. So lifeless. ... The young audience was polite, neat, plastic. It was all so phoney, and the people were eating it up. Then I switched over to Humphrey and watched him destroy everything he once stood for, trying on his new image,

Opposite: *A political party. Onset with Natalie Wood*
Following page: *Campaigning in the street Both from* The Candidate

96

and I resented him. He also had this strange end-of-the-line fatigue, and I thought to myself, this would make a movie. So I started to research it. I went to the Kennedy archives, to Senators, TV announcers and political columnists to get the feel of it. . . .'

He wanted Michael Ritchie for director again. Ritchie, who had himself campaigned for the liberal-minded John Tunney, was eager to do it. He and Redford hired Jeremy Larner, who had been one of Eugene McCarthy's speech-writers, to produce a script. The overall idea, according to Ritchie, was to dramatise the political rise of 'someone like Ralph Nader or Jerry Brown, the kind of guy who hates politics, thinks it's all bullshit, then gets involved in it'.

Bill McKay (Redford) is someone just like that. The son of a former Californian Senator, he is a civil rights-inclined lawyer, young, good-looking, and involved in all the right kind of causes. He has no political ambitions.

Marvin Lucas (Peter Boyle), professional wheeler-dealer and political packager, has other ideas. His party needs a candidate for the upcoming election; there is not much hope of turning out the incumbent Senator Jarmon (Don Porter), but there is every need to keep the party machine in employment and perks. He comes to McKay with the film's keynote speech: 'You're happy? OK. Clams are happy. You saved some trees, you got a clinic opened. Does that make you feel

The moment of triumph. The Candidate

101

102

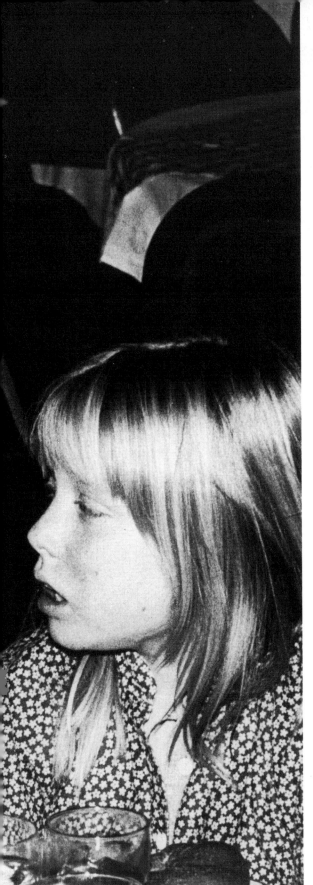

good? Meanwhile, Jarmon sits on his committees and carves up the land, the oil, the taxes....' Lucas tells McKay that he's bound to lose, so there'll be no need for him to compromise any of his beliefs. On the other hand, he will have the use of the candidate's platform for nine months in which to espouse those beliefs. McKay can't deny the logic and agrees to stand, provided that he is left free to speak his mind, and that his father's name is not invoked in his support.

These good intentions gradually ebb away. McKay's forthrightness, to everyone's surprise, starts winning potential votes, and victory begins to seem a possibility. The time for compromises has arrived, and McKay proves willing, albeit reluctantly, to make them. He rushes to the scene of a forest fire in search of media exposure, only to be beaten by Jarmon's arrival in a helicopter. Television commercials turn McKay's candour into the required all-thing-to-all-people garbage. He gets his father's endorsement. Then, at a televised debate which he has himself demanded, McKay not only avoids all the substantive issues but actually has the nerve to accuse his opponent of avoiding them. It proves a master-stroke. He wins, and is left muttering 'what do we do now?' to Lucas. His forthrightness has become just an image of forthrightness, his concern just an image of concern. It is another empty Redford victory.

Parallels with *Downhill Racer* run right through the movie. The basic theme of the

Redford with his daughter, Shauna

cost of winning, the secondary theme of the media as imagifier, and Ritchie's terse, semi-documentary style, rich in detail and immediacy, all echo the earlier film. Again there is the performer's relationships with coach and girlfriend/wife, again the semi-reluctant winner slowly intoxicated by his own success. But the subject-matter is more portentous, and, as a result, the second film tends to focus less on the individual and more on the system. *The Candidate* is a film about democracy, or what passes for it in the United States, and as the audience watches the steady, relentless corruption of McKay's idealism, it is in effect being asked: 'what hope is there with such a political system?'

This question is not posed directly by the film, let alone satisfactorily answered. It could be argued, of course, that raising the relevant issues is enough. Or that commercial cinema could not go further and remain commercial. But such arguments seem like a cop-out. By painting such a bleak picture of the democratic process, and by avoiding the raising of alternative scenarios, the message of *The Candidate*—and it is a film which can't avoid having a message—is reduced to a distaste for the whole notion of politics.

One reviewer thought the film's makers 'assume that the movie-going electorate will take the corrupting and deadening weight of the political machine as a fact of life, so that the film can dodge the morality of the debate and more cynically annotate the detail'. This seems harsh, but in terms of the final product it also seems justified. *The Candidate* reinforced public cynicism, without advancing public understanding of the reasons for such a corrupting state of affairs one iota. The film condemned the Jarmons of this world, and then showed that the McKays can only win by becoming Jarmons. All these Jarmons would continue to carve up 'the land, the oil, the taxes', and, deep down, the people who made *The Candidate* seemed to believe that there was no democratic way of stopping them. This tied in with Redford's own belief in individual action, and his corresponding disbelief in social action. He and they may have been right—may still be right—but if so should he and they not have been making, or trying to make, movies which explored other types of democracy or other political modes of action? Making *The Candidate* only made sense in the way clearing a piece of land makes sense—in terms of what is to be built in the space which is cleared.

This is perhaps unfair. Any film which annoys politicians as much as *The Candidate* did in 1972 must have something going for it.

The price of popcorn

Jeremiah Johnson and *The Candidate*, both released in 1972, were to be the last movies Redford 'felt a passion for' for several years. In the period 1972–5 he was to star in six other films, which can be roughly broken into two categories—four 'caper' films and two 'matinee idol blockbusters'. This period was to mark a consolidation of his star-appeal, a development of his talents as an actor pure and simple, and an artistic—in the wider sense—standstill.

Comments from him and George Roy Hill (director of *The Sting* and *The Great Waldo Pepper*) are indicative of the level of thought and artistic commitment which went into the four 'caper' films. Redford said of *The Hot Rock* (*How To Steal A Diamond In Four Uneasy Lessons* in the UK): 'I wanted to do a caper film just for the fun of it. And I wanted to work with an ensemble group of actors.' Plus he needed the money—'I was flat broke—really had financial problems at the time. It's the only film I've ever done with money as a principal consideration.' As for *The Sting*, its eventual niche in cinematic history was suggested by George Roy Hill in one line: 'I liked it and I thought it would be good as a filler until I could start to do *Waldo Pepper*.' This latter film Redford made 'for fun. Like *The Sting*. It has no message. It should be very entertaining and have a sense of style, adventure and romance.' *Three Days of the Condor*, Redford told eventual director Pollack, was 'bullshit, but it's the kind of picture we've always talked about wanting to do where you don't have to worry about the meaning of this and the meaning of that. It's a popcorn movie, a thriller. You'll see when you read it, it goes

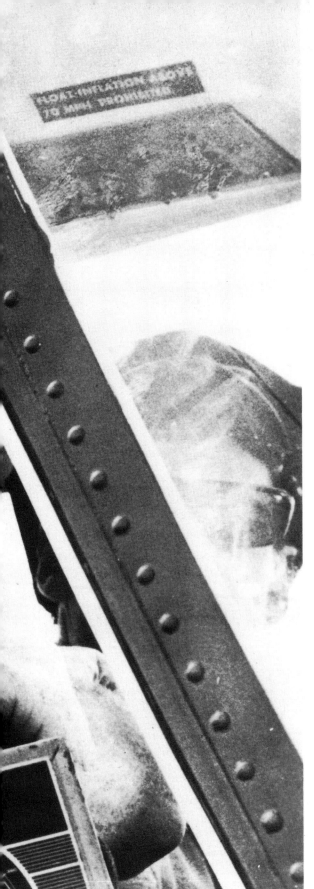

like the wind.'

Entertainment is a much-abused word. According to one dictionary, to entertain is to 'amuse, to provide pleasant diversion'. Sounds harmless enough, and indeed the words 'harmless fun' crop up with amazing regularity in reviews of these and other like-'minded' films. The 'caper' movie has come to specialise in the absence of anything likely to make an audience think or feel. Its aims are to be 'crisp and stylish' (review of *The Hot Rock*), a 'lightweight delight' (*The Sting*), or 'eminently satisfying just as a spectacle' (*The Great Waldo Pepper*).

Yet these are important films, for the simple reason that many people see them. Through their celebration of certain values (or the lack of them) such films form a vital part of the processes by which our society reflects on itself, and by which it confirms or denies it prejudices. For every person being urged to question by a film like, say, *The Battle of Algiers*, there are a hundred being urged not to by films like *The Sting*. And for every fun-film, like *Flash Gordon*, which seeks only to 'amuse' and 'divert', there are many more pushing unspoken and unthought-out values down the throats of their diverted audiences.

What, after all, is the basic emotional force motivating the heroes of *Butch Cassidy*, *The Hot Rock* and *The Sting*? Criminal greed. The illicit pursuit of money and more money. In each movie this central motive force is masked by an elaborate series of plot-devices. In *Butch Cassidy* it is

As Dortmunder, dropping in on the police in How to Steal a Diamond in Four Uneasy Lessons *(1972)*

the blurring, metaphorically and literally, of everyone but the heroes, in *The Hot Rock* the effect is achieved by creating a spurious confusion as to the diamond's rightful owners (if it doesn't really belong to the African nation which has it, then what could be wrong with stealing it?); in *The Sting* by the equally spurious murder of Hooker's mentor and the disguising of the theft as a 'con', a form of artistic endeavour.

In each film the audience is forced squarely behind the criminals—they are cleverer, more charming, and they are played by the stars. They also make the foolish mistakes, so that we can empathise with their human frailty. They get the women too, such as they are; in films like these womankind is at best irrelevant, at worst an updated Neanderthal fantasy. They are there to service the buddy-buddy heroes, to speed them on their adolescent way. The men have to have the women to prove that they're 'normal', and they have to treat them like dirt to prove that they're men. It is no surprise that the most vociferous fans of such movies are adolescent males (of all ages).

The values these films cart around are the only thing about them which is real. The plots are ludicrous, and generally full of holes. Where in *The Sting* is the world of the Great Depression? Where is any genuine sense of the criminal underworld spawned by economic crisis? Redford is too old for his part, Newman too young for his. Only the clothes are right; even the 'period' music comes from the wrong period.

It could be said of these particular films that they at least refrain from indulging in gratuitously violent sex or gratuitously gory violence. But this is just as calcu-lated—it is what makes them 'family entertainment', what gets them prime-time television slots a couple of years after release. And the family is just as corrupted. The Goldman/Hill vision of adolescence run amok has no more, and probably less, claim to moral rectitude than the most cold-hearted of Eastwood or Bronson's film output. *Dirty Harry* and his ilk at least confront their audience head on, whereas Goldman and Hill seek to seduce and charm their audience into the same spot at the heart of an amoral universe.

Of course, these films do provide entertainment. *The Hot Rock* has some fine playing by the 'ensemble', some very funny moments, and its characters are not drawn only as misplaced angels. *The Sting*, though overly drawn out and mechanically contrived, has a brilliant twist ending. It is *The Great Waldo Pepper* which seems to lack any redeeming qualities. Here Hill and Goldman reach their apotheosis, creating a movie which is both tasteless and offensive, and which also lacks charm or wit. At the superficial level the central character is another Chappellet or McKay, obsessed with winning something, but where the Redford/Ritchie and Pollack/Redford partnerships have often managed to create complex characters whose uncertainty balanced their ambition, the Goldman/Hill/Redford trio here conjures up only an ugly American idol.

Waldo Pepper is a 'barnstormer' in the twenties, an ex-First World War pilot who

Opposite: *Dortmunder*
Following page: *Discussing the pay-off. With George Segal and Moses Gunn*
Both *from* How to Steal a Diamond in Four Uneasy Lessons

travels through rural America giving flying exhibitions for a living. He has two ambitions, to perform an 'outside loop' manoeuvre and to pit his skills against the legendary German air ace Ernst Kessler (Bo Brundin). The film opens with him arriving in some small rural community, only to discover competition from another 'barnstormer', Axel Olsson (Bo Svenson). Waldo cunningly removes the screws from Olsson's wheels, and in the resultant crash Olsson breaks a leg. Waldo then collects money from the crowd, ostensibly for his injured 'partner', and walks off with it himself.

But does the audience assume from this that Pepper is a nasty piece of work? Oh no—because Olsson has not been presented as a sympathetic character, because Waldo takes a freckled-faced lad up in his plane as a treat, because he is wearing a white shirt, and because he has the captivating Redford grin. How could an audience turn against such charm?

As the movie progresses, through the odd fatal accident and Waldo's grounding by the authorities, the audience is never invited to question Waldo's methods or ambitions. The nobility of the fliers, like the nobility of the outlaws in *Butch Cassidy*, is pitted against the faceless kill-joys of authority and the mass of humanity as self-seeking morons, whose only reaction to a plane crash is to scramble for souvenirs while the pilot screams in agony. Goldman's script crackles along, putting down anyone and anything which doesn't share in the fliers' adolescent fantasies.

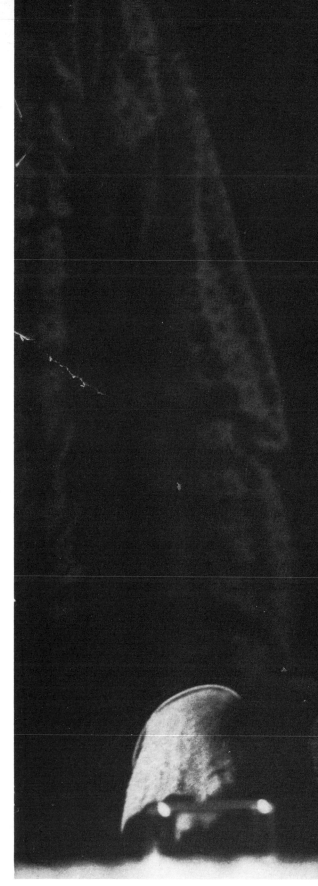

The Sting *(1973)*

2062.38

When Waldo and Kessler eventually fight it out in the sky above a film set, the message is anything but ambivalent. These men are something special, heroes even.

Paulene Kael put it succinctly: 'I can't tell if Americans will like this movie, but I think Hitler would have drunk a toast to it.' *Waldo Pepper* has its blond Aryan hero, drunk on combat as a rite of purification, oblivious to other people as anything more than a testing-ground for his own version of manliness. 'Are you going to license the clouds?' he bursts out, when told he needs a licence for flying. With people like him opposing the idea, you begin to feel it must have some merit.

Three Days of the Condor is also a fantasy film, but of a very different type. For one thing, the hero, a guy-mixed-up-in-some-thing-he-doesn't-understand type figure, has a reasonable enough ambition—survival. For another, the 'fantasy' had more than a modicum of contemporary relevance.

Joseph Turner (Redford) riffles through pulp fiction in search of ideas which might prove useful to his CIA bosses. Returning from the take-away one day with his co-workers' lunch he discovers them all dead. For the rest of the film he seeks both to avoid their fate and find some reason for it. In the process he is forced to abduct Kathy Hale (Faye Dunaway), whose apartment is plastered with photographs of leafless

Opposite: *Two's company, three's a bust*
Following pages: *Hooker and Gondorff (Paul Newman) and a lucky strike*
All from The Sting

115

2062. 55

trees and empty park benches. They become lovers (in the one sequence of the movie which defies all credibility), and she helps him in his search for explanation and survival.

Three Days of the Condor is reasonably superior popcorn. It entertains without totally numbing or warping the mind. The tension is well sustained, and the action does not depend for its excitement on measuring out blood by the quart. Redford and Dunaway are convincing enough; Cliff Robertson and Max Von Sydow, as malignant cynicism and cynical malignance respectively, provide solid back-up. There is no sledgehammer moralising, no happy cut-and-dried ending.

Of course, it is always easier to create sympathy for characters who don't know what is happening, than it is for characters, like Waldo, who think they know everything and in fact know next to nothing. But Pollack and Redford have never gone in for the plot-rigged glorification of the resourceful hero which directors like George Roy Hill seem to find so satisfying. *Three Days* is no exception; it is about people as well as images and plot, and it doesn't need the glamorous grins or the charming wisecracks to create a genuine bond between its protagonists. It is a story, not a myth twisted for commercial convenience. If, in the end, *Three Days* is not much more than simple entertainment, then so be it. The trouble with *The Sting* and *Waldo Pepper* is that they offer more than that; they also seek to extol a

Previous page: *Offset during the shooting of* The Great Waldo Pepper *(1975)*
Opposite and following pages: *Further shots from* The Great Waldo Pepper. *With the wounded hero is Margot Kidder*

121

2069-

version of American heroism which, for all its box office appeal, is morally bankrupt.

As for Redford, he seemed to fit into either world, as the Aryan outdoor Waldo or the bookish, uncertain Turner. This was not just a matter of acting ability; it was also a great part of Redford's appeal to the seventies. As the previous decade had celebrated the twin gods of change and non-commitment, so the back-lash featured a devotion to conservation—in both the conservative and conservationist senses—and to commitment, whether to ideas, goals or other people. Redford's characters, and to some extent Redford himself, were perfect representatives for this back-lash. They were conservatives with a small 'c', looking nostalgically back upon the past, and looking sour-eyed at the present and future. Yet they were also all committed to one thing or another, and it was this fierce sense of loyalty, to a partner or an idea, which gave them their emotional resonance. What is attractive about Butch and Sundance, or about Gondorff and Hooker in *The Sting*, is this loyalty. The only time the heartstrings are really pulled in the latter film is when you find out that they have not betrayed each other, when you have been led to think that they have.

The unfortunate corollary of the sixties' emphasis on change and non-commitment was an epidemic of selfishness posing as liberty; the problem with the seventies' back-lash has been a retreat into narrow-mindedness. In most of his films the Redford persona has managed to steer clear of this, through both the repeated expressions of self-doubt and the pyrrhic nature of his successive victories. Only in *Waldo Pepper* was this commitment to 'no change', to the rolling back of time in favour of the obsolete 'barnstormers' and their Prussian attitudes, allowed to become total. Then the character became unpleasantly totalitarian. Conservation, loyalty, commitment—all have to reach beyond the self to be human, and Waldo was unaware that a world existed beyond himself.

Not-so-friendly competition. With Bo Svenson in The Great Waldo Pepper
Following page: *Extracting the truth, a scene from* Three Days of the Condor *(1975)*

124

The matinee idol (with feet of clay)

By 1973 Redford was one of the premier romantic/sex symbols on the Hollywood roster. This was somewhat surprising, if only for the fact that he hadn't played a traditional romantic leading man role since *This Property is Condemned*, way back in pre-superstar days. It seemed high time that Sundance *et al.* alighted from their horses, skis, bikes and whatever, and had a sustained shot at a long-term relationship with a real female character.

The script for *The Way We Were* had been written by Arthur Laurents as a vehicle for Barbra Streisand. He and producer Ray Stark picked on Pollack to direct, and Pollack, conscious of the need for a strong presence to counter-balance Streisand's— 'she'd been running all over her leading men'—picked on Redford to play the male lead. But the latter was less than willing. 'Aw, that piece of junk' he replied to Pollack's initial enquiry. 'Yeah, they sent it to me a long time ago in treatment form. I passed.'

But to Redford's amazement, Pollack persisted. He couldn't see anything in either the character or the story. 'What is this picture about, Pollack?' he asked. 'What is this guy? He's just an object . . . he's a nothing . . . he runs around saying, "aw, c'mon Katie, c'mon Katie." He doesn't do anything . . . she wants everything. What does this guy want, Pollack? WHAT DOES HE WANT?'

But he agreed to do it eventually. 'I had faith that Pollack would make something more out of the character than was in the original script. Had I not had faith in Sydney and myself and David Rayfiel and Alvin Sargent working together to create

130

Previous page: *A tearful reunion*
Opposite: *Katie and Hubbell*
Following page: *Katie tries to instil Hubbell with ambition*
All from The Way We Were *(1973)*

some kind of depth to the character, I wouldn't have taken the role. As it was written, he was shallow and one-dimensional. Not very real—more a figment of someone's imagination of what Prince Charming should be like. What emerged from the rewrites were glimpses of the darker side of this golden boy character— what his fears were about himself. The idea was to create a supposed Mr Perfect but then give little hints along the way that everything wasn't so perfect—or that he, more importantly, knew it wasn't.'

The Way We Were was intended to be an old-style romantic melodrama, man and woman joining together and falling apart to the accompaniment of the string section and much muffled sobbing in the back stalls. But it would also be something more; this particular 'love story' would be interwoven with developments in American politics during the decade or so straddling the end of the Second World War, carrying its protagonists through from the bright-eyed innocence of pre-war college to the dark paranoia of anti-communist witch-hunts in Hollywood. The film's makers could not be faulted for lack of ambition.

At the beginning of *The Way We Were* Katie Morosky (Streisand) comes across her erstwhile college contemporary Hubbell Gardiner (Redford) perched drunkenly on a New York barstool. An extended flashback then recounts the story of their college days, with Katie as the effervescent communist agitator, her life devoted to the

Opposite: *'Why doesn't she shut up?'*
Following page: *One of the happy times*
Both from The Way We Were

135

Cause and nothing but the Cause, and Hubbell as the all-American boy—'America the Beautiful' as she sarcastically dubs him—outwardly self-assured and disinclined to take politics seriously. It had been a case of opposites attracting despite themselves, but that attraction has never, until now—we are back in the present—been consummated. The romance proceeds to grow, the war years slip behind, and the now-married couple move to Hollywood where Hubbell is adapting his novel for the cinema and Katie is still being Katie. The same chemistry which pulls them together is forever threatening to pull them apart, and the bulk of the film follows this psychic tug-o-war through to its inevitable and weepy conclusion.

The Way We Were is not short on faults. The plot, for a start, is often hard to follow, with time passing at either a gallop or a snail's pace and with nothing to indicate which. More disturbing to some reviewers was what they considered a pro-communist slant to the movie. By making Katie the more sympathetic character—she is more entranced by the relationship when it's going well, more deeply hurt when it isn't, and she's played by Streisand—the audience is inevitably drawn, so the argument went, into identifying with her communist viewpoint. This is also made easier by the absence of any other activism for audience consideration. The only countervailing forces are Hubbell's passive cynicism and the offstage machinations of the powers-that-be.

It could well be argued that there's nothing wrong with Katie's views, particularly in the matter of Hollywood blacklisting. But quite apart from this, the argument is false, because Hubbell does stand for something considerably more potent than passive cynicism. He had been re-written to fit Redford, and in many ways he emerges as the archetypal Redford character, encompassing all those contradictions which had bedevilled his predecessors.

Who is Hubbell Gardiner? For once we find out quite a lot about a single Redford character, and by implication about the other Redford characters. The Hubbell-his friends-Katie triangle throws light on the Sundance-Butch-Etta triangle, emphasising the extent to which the Redford persona is forever torn between adolescence and responsibility. In the way Hubbell deals with Hollywood's attempt to 'commercialise' his book, the suspected failure of an elected Senator McKay to rise above the prevailing corruption receives a depressing confirmation. We even have, straight from Hubbell's mouth, several terse statements of the Redford persona's credo.

'Like the country he lived in, everything came easy to him. But at least he knew it.' So begins Hubbell's college essay. When Katie asks him, after he has been unfaithful to her, whether he is 'still a nice gentile boy?', he replies: 'No. And I never was. That was your idea of me.' Hubbell has seen through his own myth, and has acquired a potent mistrust of the myths of others, personal or political. To him, a pragmatic self-awareness, and a determination to deal with what *is*, are more important, more real.

After rescuing Katie from a bunch of commie-bashers in the Union Station

Opposite: *Hubbell and Katie in California*
Following page: *After the consummation*
Both from The Way We Were

7530.

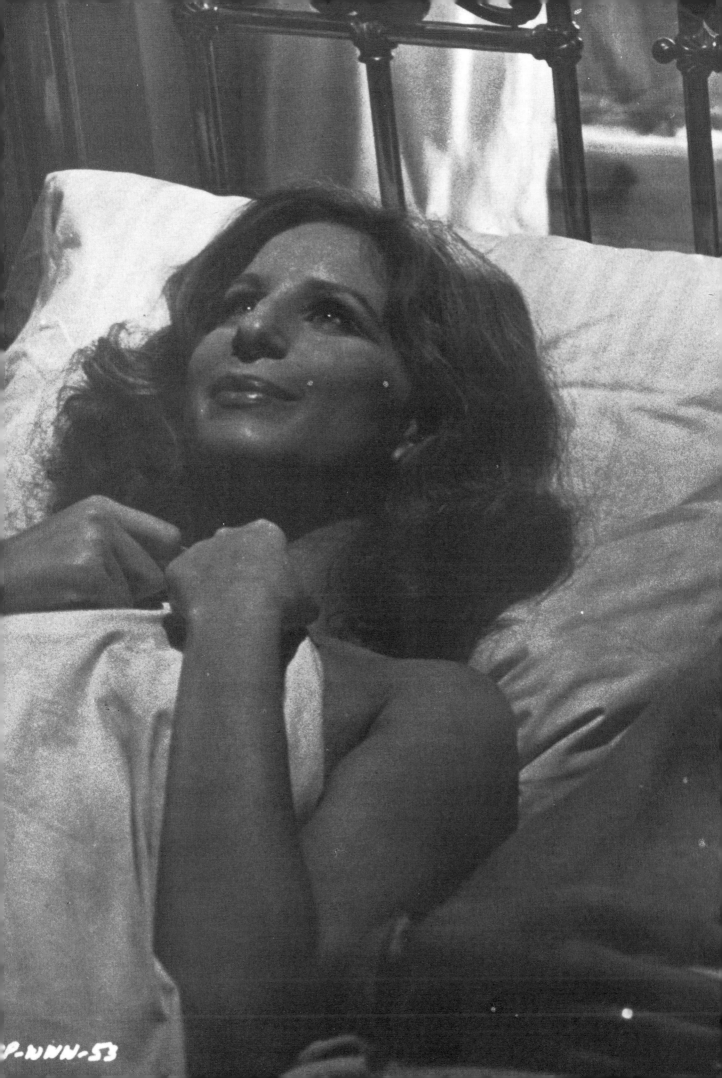

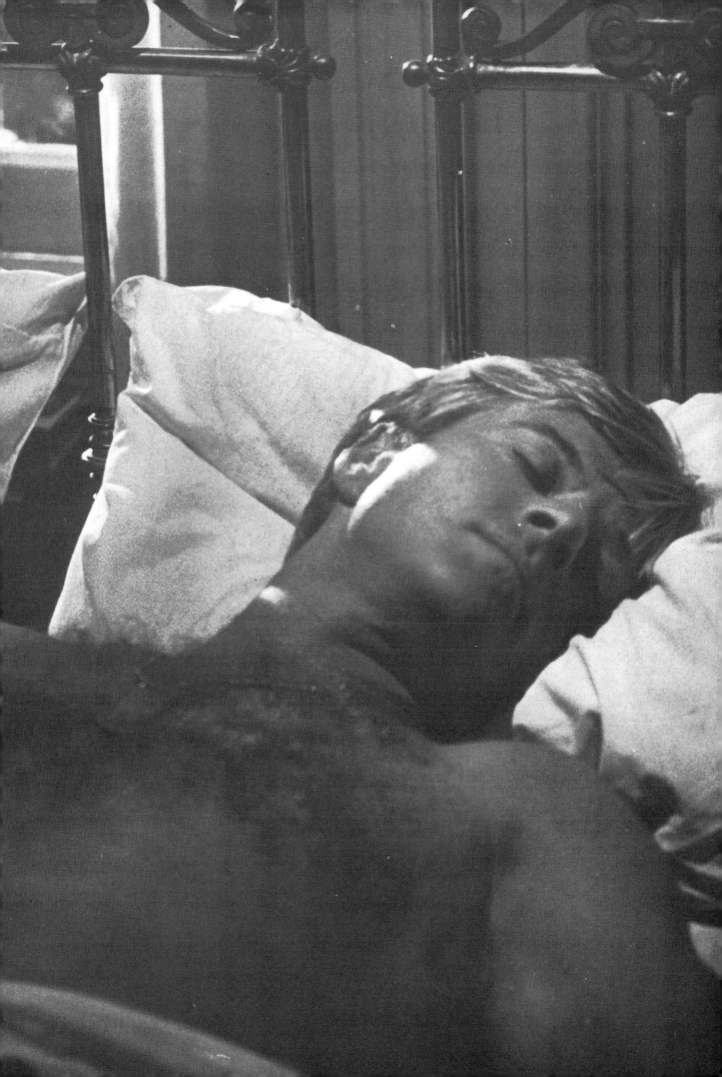

concourse he tells her: 'This isn't college, Katie, it's grown-up politics, it's stupid and dangerous.' When she counter-accuses him of unwillingness to make a stand for what he believes in, he replies: 'I'm trying to tell you that people are more important than any goddam witch-hunt. People! You and me. Not principles.'

It is not that Hubbell favours the status quo. 'We don't have free speech in this country and we never will' he says at one point. But this doesn't mean that demanding it will make any difference. 'Nothing will change.' Nothing will come out of Katie's campaign against McCarthyism except problems for Katie and himself. In a few years McCarthy will be gone, and the writers and film-makers will then be able to say what they can't say now. Getting black-listed is not going to help anybody.

So Hubbell endures the slow castration of his book by the studio, devoting his efforts to saving what can be saved from the wreckage of its commercialisation. He will not simply throw in the towel by taking on what can't be beaten. He will not be paralysed in opposition. It's a sell-out, of course, but at least he knows that that is what he's doing. His inner integrity is not being put at risk. It's Sheriff Cooper hunting down Willie Boy all over again; he knows it's wrong, which doesn't make it right, but which does keep it at a distance from his real self. What is the alternative? Tilting at windmills, a retreat into ideology, into myth, into compromising the self in a different way, all without hope of success? The powers-that-be are too powerful to be confronted, and too certain of their power to be reasoned with.

This is a valid point of view. It is not mere cynicism. It reflects one of the lessons learned in the sixties, that huffing and puffing is unlikely to blow their house down. But it is also a confused point of view, resting as it does on the dubious supposition that the powers-that-be will leave the Hubbells of this world the space they need in which to preserve their true selves. It is, of course, easier for people with mountain kingdoms to believe as much, but even Redford admits to having no real answers. Hubbell certainly has none. He is an essentially sad figure, prepared to hang on to what is wrong because he sees no hope of putting it right. Such a viewpoint begs all the questions, but at least it is the right questions which are being begged. *The Way We Were* was one of a select band of seventies' films which managed to bridge, however tenuously, the growing chasm between massive commercial success and a thoughtful exploration of human relationships in both the personal and social context.

The Great Gatsby was not so fortunate. Fitzgerald's book had been filmed before with a conspicuous lack of success, but by the early seventies the Siamese relationship between Vietnam and Nixonian skullduggery was driving America, and its cinema industry, into the past in search of solace. *The Way We Were* was one example of this trend, and, so the logic went, if a piece of custom-made nostalgia like that could do so well, then what price one of the masterpieces of American literature? To the business mind, there seemed no reason why it should not be, at last, translated

'America the Beautiful'. The Way We Were

© CRWW-15

SCH- GG - 1394

into one of the (best-selling) masterpieces of the American cinema.

The businessmen did not instigate the move, though. This honour belonged to actress Ali McGraw, who besides harbouring a compulsive desire to play the character of Daisy, also happened to be the wife of Paramount production chief Bob Evans. He went to Broadway producer David Merrick, and Merrick tried to purchase the screen rights from Fitzgerald's daughter. He was not alone in this endeavour—both Ray Stark and Redford himself were also interested—and as a result it took Paramount eighteen months and $350,000 plus percentage to clinch the deal.

The search for someone to play Gatsby proved no easier. Warren Beatty and Jack Nicholson were both approached, and both refused to work with the unpopular McGraw. Brando was then offered the role, but he wanted too much money. Finally, Redford was invited to grasp the nettle, which he willingly did.

The directors proved equally loth to work with McGraw. Peter Bogdanovich, Arthur Penn and Mike Nichols all reportedly declined the assignment, which eventually went to the British director Jack Clayton. He found there was no screenplay to work with. This job had been given to Truman Capote, and his version of Gatsby turned out to be less than straight. Gay Gatsbys, as all production chiefs know all too well, do not make a great American picture. Capote's script was rejected, its author handsomely

Previous pages: *Daisy and Jay. With Mia Farrow*
Opposite: *With Sam Waterston*
Both from The Great Gatsby *(1974)*

146

147

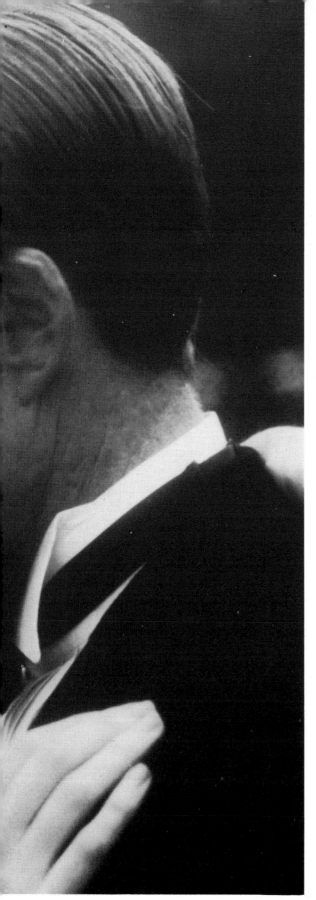

compensated, and Francis Ford Coppola was asked to write a new one.

Then a problem arose. Ali McGraw's marriage to Bob Evans had broken on the bow of her love-match with *Getaway* co-star Steve McQueen, and the latter was reluctant to let McGraw play Daisy if he couldn't play Gatsby. Since McQueen didn't fit anyone's idea of Gatsby, McGraw withdrew, leaving the picture Daisyless. It was eventually decided, after another exhaustive selection process, that Mia Farrow would best fill the role.

After all this the movie had to be a hit, and Paramount were to leave no stone unturned in their attempt to assure as much. The publicity machine was cranked into over-drive. America was to be 'Gatsbyised'; the clothes, the hairstyles, even a variety of Teflon cookware—all were to be transported by time warp from the thirties and sold, along with the movie, to a nostalgia-hungry nation. Evans announced, in one of those ringing sentences which make Europeans wonder if there is hope for America, that 'the making of a blockbuster is the newest art form of the twentieth century'.

Somewhere amidst this hype-happy wing-ding a movie was being made. Redford had 'wanted Gatsby badly. He is not fleshed out in the book, and the implied parts of his character are fascinating. ... It was a chance to elude a stereotyped image.' Some chance. Redford was, for once, being naive if he thought the block-buster Paramount had in mind could

Previous pages and opposite: The Great Gatsby *with Mia Farrow*

GG-R-35

accommodate the sort of film he wanted made. One or the other was bound to disappear. The public was being prepared for a glossy love story, and the creative team was busy trying to fashion a good film from a book which was notoriously difficult to translate into cinematic terms.

Sure enough there was no blockbuster: without the pre-sales drummed up by the publicity machine the movie would have been a commercial disaster. Redford was accused of awkward speech and looking too good by critics who had expected a sensation and found only a reasonably faithful rendition of Fitzgerald. This surprised Redford. '*Fitzgerald* never said Gatsby wasn't good-looking. He said Gatsby was a fine figure of a man, an elegant young roughneck. He said Gatsby's language was awkward, bordering on the absurd. That was the key to the character. That was the quality I *worked* for. I mean, didn't they read the *book*?'

Of course they didn't. The film was far too good for its own publicity, well acted by an exceptionally strong cast (Redford, Bruce Dern, Farrow, Karen Black, Sam Waterston, Lois Chiles, Scott Wilson), and coming as close to Fitzgerald's ambience as anyone could hope. It deserved better than cookware tie-ins.

Redford was naturally disappointed. The experience had been 'like robbing a bank and discovering you took the wrong bag'. But really he had no one to blame but himself for getting mixed up in the whole business. As he said himself, 'the fact that Paramount approached Marlon really makes you wonder'. It should have done.

Previous pages: The Great Gatsby

154

PART FOUR

An Artist from Utah

All The President's Men
A Bridge Too Far
The Electric Horseman
Brubaker
Ordinary People

The beleaguered American

WITH *The Way We Were* and *The Sting* breaking box office records around the cinematised world, and with the Gatsby hype breaking all records in badly judged salesmanship, the decade passed its half-way point with Redford's star shining at

157

its brightest. His buddy-buddy roles apparently pleased the male audience, his flawed Prince Charming role in *The Way We Were* apparently captivated the other half of civilised humanity. His conservative-style rebellion managed to please most conservatives and most rebels, with only the entrenched powers of the establishment and revolution finding reason for dislike. He seemed to appeal to almost everyone. He was, in Michael Wood's words, 'the square, conventional American boy who turns out to be more interesting than he seems to have any right to be. He is a victory both for conventional America and for its enemies, a man for all American seasons.'

In the same article Wood noted that stardom in films is essentially 'a story, an embryonic tale carried from movie to movie'. Redford's story, through from Sundance to Hubbell Gardiner, had carried him right along the same mainstream channel which his nation had travelled. His characters were anti-establishment, but not because they harboured any hopes of effecting change; they were as aware of the limits of change as they were of the limits of the status quo. Within that realisation they sought to preserve their own freedom of movement, by being aware of what had to be done and then doing it. Compromise was no longer a dirty word, as long as the character was aware of how and why he was compromising.

Redford's main problem with this persona was its tendency towards blandness, towards, in fact, its 'man-for-all-seasons' lack of a real cutting edge. This problem was complicated by the star image—the blue eyes and flashing grin—which typed him as a traditional Hollywood hero-figure, the sort of man who had no right to be bland, who was supposed to have answers, to be decisive and completely succesful. Thus David Thomson could write that 'cinemas are clotted with his effacing handsomeness.... It is a perfect fit of periods that he should inhabit the hollow shell of the Great Gatsby. ... Fitzgerald's fascinating lacuna turned into this decade's archetypal hollow man.'

Redford himself seemed partially aware of this problem. 'I never thought of myself as a glamorous guy or even a particularly handsome guy. But suddenly I have this image and it makes me nervous. Critics are no longer able to judge my performances. My looks seem to keep getting in the way.' But this was hardly just the critics' fault. The way Pollack lingers over Hubbell's handsome features in *The Way We Were* asks for such criticism; if the character is to be taken as more than a romantic symbol then he must be filmed as more. In all three George Roy Hill films Redford's good looks are almost a part of the plot, giving substance to the 'charm' that makes the films 'work'.

Redford was more concerned with the way his image was being manipulated away from the film set. 'I kept encountering my likeness on television, on magazine covers, even in comic strips. It was always slightly distorted, larger than life. I was alarmed by the size of the image that was emerging at that time.' His director for *Little Fauss and Big Halsy*, Sidney J. Furie, had pinpointed the reason why Redford, more than other stars, should find this so

At the New York Cosmos' farewell soccer game for Pelé

158

disturbing. He was 'unlike any other actor I'd ever met. If you didn't know he was an actor because you recognised him you'd think he was a young executive. He's personable, matter-of-fact, no bullshit, no small-talk, no talking about girls or drinking or what he did last night. . . . You know there's a certain unreality about acting. But Redford's the realest actor I've ever met. He's just a guy who happens to be an actor. It's his work, and that's where it starts and ends.'

At least, that's where Redford would have liked it to start and end. But of course it didn't. The public, or at least some of it, wanted more than a screen image; it wanted to know what lay behind the grin, what was ticking away under the straw mop. As a result Redford found himself in a shrinking capsule. 'Walking down the street, I feel I'm in a head-on collision, that my life is getting narrower and narrower and I wonder why I'm so uptight. I've lost the capacity to wander around anonymously, just hanging out, being loose, watching people and listening to them.' The days in Europe, almost twenty years before, had by this time acquired an enormous significance. They stood for the freedom that success had cost him, probably forever.

By the mid-seventies the pressures had grown to an almost intolerable level, and the yearning to live at least some facets of an ordinary life had become intense. He was fed up with 'people making a big deal of fuss' over him, fed up with 'looking as if I know what I'm doing'. He wanted to get away from those 'who see me as having the temperament of the Sundance Kid, the charm of the Candidate, the sense of humour of *The Sting* and the wardrobe of the Great Gatsby'.

More than ever he could afford to get away. In Utah he could forget the public and the media, 'build a solar house, write a book, farm, watch my kids grow . . . enjoy the things I worked for'. He could afford to turn down lucrative parts that didn't interest him. He could afford to win auctions for material he really wanted to be involved with.

But what sort of material would this be? Stardom, and the retreat from it which has been undertaken by film stars and rock stars alike, inevitably tends to stunt the learning process. Redford was right to express dismay over his inability to 'watch people and listen to them', for locked in a cocoon partly, but only partly, of his own making, his experience of the 'real world' was inevitably restricted. And this would affect the attitudes he brought to his films.

A man who says 'crowds and groups have always made me nervous—they panic me now—just because I don't trust them' is unlikely to embrace the politics of mass action. And since only such action can democratically change things, it is natural for him to say of real change: 'I don't see that happening right away, so I'm not interested in it.' The pressures of stardom are pressures for conservatism.

But the same withdrawal also reinforced the rebel in Redford. When he says 'I rebel against any force that threatens to overwhelm me as an individual. . . . I don't like the fact that I have no opportunity to criticise the people who are in a position to make decisions that affect my life' he is talking about a wide range of forces, ranging through Nixonian government, the spoilation of his Utah backyard, the idolisation of fans. A film star, as public figure and actor, is always being called on to sacrifice his or her individuality, whether to the images of the public or the characters he or she plays. And in modern society, where the sheer complexity of life creates a situation in which the individual is no more than a statistic to all but personal acquaintances, and where decisions are constantly being made which affect every one, the film star, like every other citizen, is bogged down in a sense of social impotence. In Redford the rebel actor and the rebel citizen inevitably intertwined.

Cut off, more so than most, from that society, his rebellion was necessarily individualistic. The conservative within reinforced that choice. With no faith in social action as a curative factor, not much liking for the present as it existed outside his Utah hideaway, his faith was more and more rooted in the legendary individualism of the past, in a time when men could still make their own decisions unfettered by the decisions of others, when there was still sufficient room to make personal rebellion effective. Redford became the beleaguered American, demanding a return to the old values of honesty and personal responsibility, and lamenting a world which was lost.

Following page: *Riding with Lola*

All the President's lies

When the Watergate break-in took place in June 1972, Redford was himself on the campaign trail, doing a publicity tour for *The Candidate*. Talking to journalists he found that most of them considered such nefarious activities came under the heading of business-as-usual in Washington. Whoever was responsible was unlikely to pay.

Consequently, he was more than impressed by the dirt-digging activities of the two *Washington Post* reporters, Carl Bernstein and Bob Woodward. He was also struck by the contrasting personalities of the pair. Thinking that the subject might make a film, he got in touch with Woodward, who told him that a book—later published as *All The President's Men*—was in the first stages of preparation. It was apparently at Redford's suggestion that the two reporters structured the story around themselves, and wrote a 'how we uncovered it' book. Redford meanwhile was purchasing the screen rights.

He had never liked Nixon. 'He was my Senator when I was growing up in California and I never believed a word he said. It was purely intuitive, because I had no interest in politics. To me, politics was a bunch of people in suits, with no faces. Worst of all was Nixon. I'm sensitive to people's vibes. Nixon gave me an athletic award when I was thirteen and when I shook his hand, I felt absolutely nothing. That hit me, and around that time when I would see him on TV, nothing came across. I didn't believe him, it was just empty. What I couldn't understand was why as a kid with no real knowledge of politics, I felt such a strong vibration of

insincerity and why other people, especially the press, couldn't feel it. ... So when I heard a lot of political press talking about the fact that Watergate could be tied to Nixon, I not only believed it, I *wanted* to believe it. And when nothing was happening, I got angry. I was angry half from my own feelings and half for the system, for justice.'

The counterpoint to Nixon's villainy—and it was this which made the story so apposite for Redford—was the heroic determination of the dogged Woodward and Bernstein. Certainly they were backed by all the authority of the *Washington Post*, but it was as individual reporters that they tracked down the truth of Watergate, that they took on the awesome might of the established government. And they won. Butch would have been proud of them.

The film followed the book which followed the events, a sequence which caused difficulties for the film-makers. 'One of the problems we were going to have with *All The President's Men*,' Redford later said, 'was that people knew the outcome ... we had to convey that people were frightened ... to try and put the audience in the subjective position of being frightened is hard, especially when everyone knows that no one was killed and we already know who was guilty and who went to jail.' To solve this problem he enlisted Alan Pakula as director. He had worked with Pakula before on *Inside Daisy Clover*, and had been impressed with his directorial handling of suspense in *Klute*. 'To me that had the elements I thought were important to (*All The President's Men*). It had a psychological analysis of what was happening. It also had a great use of fear. And I had read the original script and it was rather banal, it had no fear in it, no excitement.'

All The President's Men *(1976)*

Redford had already cast himself in the role of Woodward, though without any initial enthusiasm for any acting challenge it might present. It was 'not something I would have chosen to go for in terms of exhibiting all the facets you might think you have or exercising your ability or stretching it.' But he did want the film to be made, his name as an actor meant money, so 'playing the role was a sacrificial thing to get it going'. Dustin Hoffman, though, was anything but reluctant to play the more extroverted Bernstein. 'I thought you'd never ask,' he replied to Redford's enquiry.

For some strange reason Redford picked on William Goldman to turn the book into a screenplay. Predictably enough, Goldman turned it into another study in male camaraderie—'Butch and Sundance Bring Down the Government' as one *Washington Post* wit dubbed it—and the *Post*'s editor was on the verge of pulling the plug on cooperation with the film-makers. The script was re-written, with Goldman taking inputs from most concerned. It went before the cameras in the fall of 1975.

All The President's Men turned out to be an excellent film. It works as a thriller, thanks largely to the taut and imaginative direction of Pakula, and it works as a political portrait of two vague ideologies—the light and the dark—competing for the soul of America. Like the Redford/Ritchie films it scores rather weakly as a study in character, but this had been considered both inevitable and necessary right from

Previous page: *With Dustin Hoffman as Bernstein*
Opposite: *Redford as Woodward*
Both from All The President's Men

168

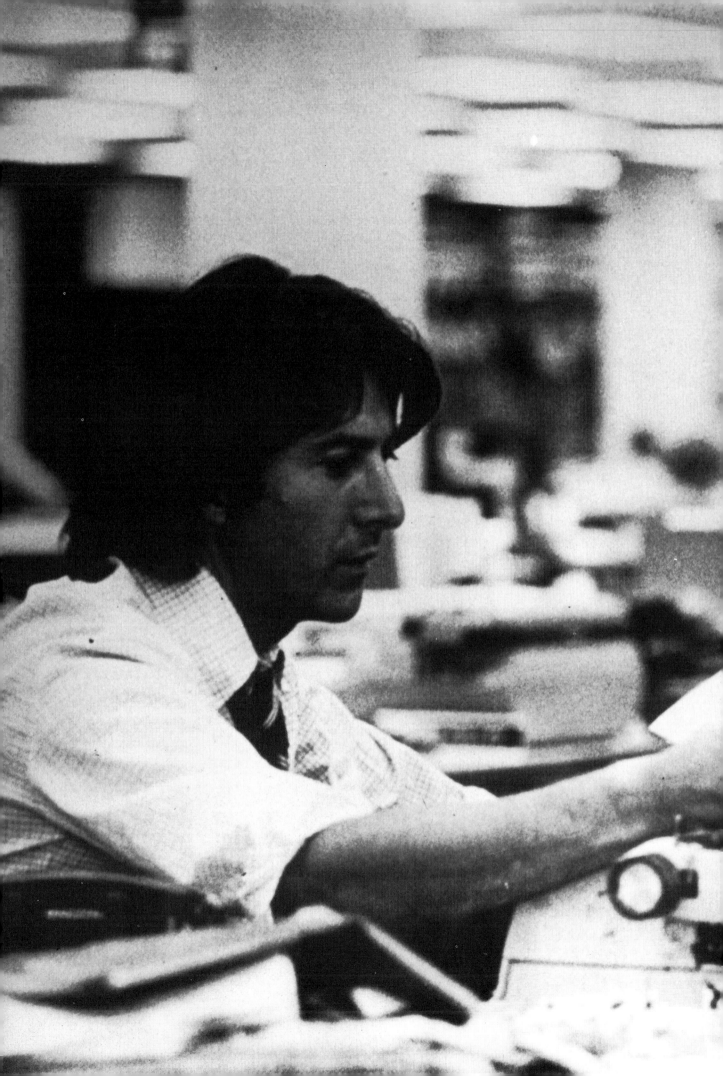

the start. 'Hype a picture like this and you lose all credibility,' Redford was to say. 'Story and atmosphere were the important things here. Character and relationships were less important. . . . I never worked on a picture that so much thought went into. A lot of it was preventive thought, not so much do this as don't do that. Don't make it a movie about Nixon or Watergate. Don't take a partisan position. Don't set out to celebrate the press. Don't be too impressed with the history involved. Don't fall in love with the *Washington Post*. Do make a movie about the press, and two reporters who did a difficult job of reporting and did it well.'

Apart from being good, the movie was also a success, grossing more than $7 million in its first week of release. Most of the critics liked it too, and Redford was, for once, happy with his own work. 'To an extent that surprises me, the movie I wanted to make is right up there on the screen: a movie about the truth, and how close we came to losing the right to know it.' It was a victory for the beleaguered American, a vindication of his belief in the individual as a still-potent factor in American society. But were Bernstein and Woodward only the exceptions which proved the rule? Redford's next two major films would offer contradictory answers to that question.

Previous page: *The truth emerges*
Opposite: *With Lola at the premier of* All The President's Men

173

174

Sundance's return

In 1976 Redford devoted three weeks to the filming of his part in *A Bridge Too Far*, the epic reconstruction of the Allied folly at Arnhem in 1944. The film had little more than size to recommend it, and Redford's decision to take part was motivated by little more than money. A 'knee-buckling' amount, as he phrased it. Well, you could hardly call $2 million for three weeks' work chicken-feed.

His next project was supposed to be *A Place To Come To*, with Sydney Pollack once more in the canvas chair. But there were problems getting it together and, according to Pollack, 'we thought we might as well do something to fill in'. The chosen filler, *The Electric Horseman*, was 'based on a script that both he and I had seen before—and both rejected. Back in the early seventies, under a different title, it had been hawked round a lot. It was a very cynical piece—in fact, the only idea we have kept is the central theme of kidnapping the horse.'

Perhaps movie-makers should make nothing but fillers. *The Sting*, for all its faults, was an infinitely better film than *Waldo Pepper*, for which it was filling in. Perhaps also, movie-makers should only take on scripts which they have previously rejected, because they then inherit the necessity for shaping story and characters into line with their own vision. The rewriting of Hubbell Gardiner's character

Rather the worse for wear. The Electric Horseman *(1978)*

175

had turned *The Way We Were* from a weepy Streisand 'vehicle' into a complex and interesting film, and the re-jigging of the newly named *Electric Horseman* script was to result in the making of one of the finest Redford/Pollack ventures.

The movie's central character—with whom Redford felt a 'direct conection'—is Sonny Steele, ex-rodeo champion, now reduced to promoting breakfast cereal for the giant AMPCO corporation. His face appears like an ikon of virility on the boxes; he travels the country, riding round arenas bedecked in lights, holding aloft an enormous illuminated cereal packet. He has become a mobile advertising hoarding, a corporate asset. The money's good, but the vibes aren't, and Sonny spends most of his time on bar-stools, arriving late and drunk for his public appearances, occasionally sliding from his saddle and into the dust with less than corporate dignity.

AMPCO has acquired another famous asset, the champion horse Rising Star. Sonny, arriving at the Las Vegas corporate convention where he and the horse are scheduled to appear together, discovers that Rising Star is pumped full of sterilising drugs. This is the last straw. When he rides the horse it is not just around the stage; he rides it right out of Las Vegas, the illuminated twosome clip-clopping down the neon tunnel like an advertisement in pursuit of liberty.

At a press conference earlier that day he has been questioned, none too sympathetically, by television reporter Hallie Martin (Jane Fonda). After his dramatic exit from the convention on Rising Star Hallie, sensing a big story and proving smarter than her rival reporters, successfully tracks him down in the wilderness. Most of the rest of the film chronicles their journey through the untamed Western landscape, to that point chosen by Sonny for setting Rising Star free. *En route* the two humans overcome their mutual distrust, but without either having to sacrifice his or her fiercely-guarded independence. She does more adjusting, but it is his world which they are travelling through. Opposites attract, particularly on cold nights in the mountains, but unlike Katie and Hubbell these two never lose sight of the fact that they belong to different worlds. It is enough to share some time together and learn something of that world which they don't belong to.

Put like this, in simplified plot form, *The Electric Horseman* sounds like a pleasant, undemanding sort of movie, relying on fashionable attitudes to give it substance and the 'chemistry' of its two stars to raise it above the mundane. Add some beguiling songs by Willie Nelson, who also acts in the film, throw in some spectacular scenery, and you can't really go wrong.

More surprisingly, the film also works at a higher level of complexity. The underlying mood—beneath the fun and frolics—is beautifully set by the sad, nostalgic Willie Nelson song which both opens and closes the movie. 'My heroes have always been cowboys' goes the refrain and never more than now, 'when the world seems to be spinning out of control'. For all its light-heartedness this is a film about sickness, about the failure of democracy and the closing of frontiers, and the plight of the individual contained therein. It is partly so

Previous page: *'My heroes have always been cowboys.' With Jane Fonda*
Opposite: *Sonny and Rising Star*
Both from The Electric Horseman

because of Fonda's presence; *The Electric Horseman* fits neatly into her canon—anti-corporate, didactic and, if not feminist, clearly conscious of sex-role stereotyping.

But the resonance of the film largely stems from Redford's presence. In a way it should have been his last film as an actor, for it completes a circle. Sonny Steele is Sundance ten years older and wiser, and *The Electric Horseman* is thus a picture of what has happened to both Redford and America in those ten years. It is a story of manipulation, image distortion, and a disillusion which refuses to become despair.

The dehumanising power of the media is, as it was in *Downhill Racer* and *The Candidate*, a strong secondary theme, explored both at the social level (Sonny versus the corporation) and at the personal level (Sonny versus Hallie and Hallie versus Hallie). But the film's main theme is the space left for, and the effectiveness of, anti-system action. Here the crucial relationship is not that between Sonny and Hallie, but that between Sonny and Rising Star. For in a sense both these 'characters' are Sundance revisited. Both are pumped full of 'drugs' at the film's beginning, both are far from their natural habitat, trapped in the warped society which feeds them. But the difference between these two Sundances is obvious. Careering along the desert roads in a van marked 'Wild Blue Yonder', only one of them is on his way to freedom. Rising Star can still be set loose; there is a valley where horses can still be horses. But for Sonny there is no such easy

Hallie and Sonny. With Jane Fonda in The Electric Horseman

180

way out anymore. He can do something 'plain and hard', he can keep 'movin' on', and so retain his sense of self, but he can do nothing to halt the conquest of the frontier by the massed forces of the sales ethic. The individual act in favour of sanity can work, but it can never be much more than an individual act, meaningful more to the person who acts than to what is acted upon. AMPCO's cereal sales go up, not down, when Sonny makes off with their asset.

Sonny Steele, The Electric Horseman

The title character of *Brubaker* is a reformist prison governor, who comes to Wakefield Prison brimming over with determination to shake things up for the better. He initially arrives as a prisoner, in order to get an inside view of the prison's *modus operandi*. He finds that the place is run for the benefit of everyone but the ordinary prisoners (the rankmen), who have to work as slave labour for local farmers and businessmen, pay for their food and health care, endure sadistic beatings and torture, and 'live' in overcrowded and decrepit conditions. However, life is not so bleak for the privileged prisoners (the trustees), the prison staff or the local businessmen. They all share in the profits, and consequently lack enthusiasm for improving the rankmen's lot.

No less obstructive is the State Prison Board, composed mostly of crooked politicians who want Wakefield Prison to be invisible, profitable and humane, in that order. Brubaker has been foisted on them by a liberal minority headed by Lillian Grey (Jane Alexander), and every reforming step he takes brings the day of his dismissal that much nearer. Eventually he discovers a graveyard of murdered prisoners, and since this threatens to rattle too many skeletons in too many closets he is fired. But in his basic goal of re-awakening the ordinary prisoners' self-respect he has succeeded. As he drives away from the prison he is showered with applause, and two years after his departure, so a written epilogue informs us, the prisoners go on to sue the state and begin the recovery of their rights.

Brubaker was directed by Stuart Rosen-

berg (taking over at an early stage from Bob Rafelson), and bears obvious resemblances to his earlier *Cool Hand Luke*. There is the same attention to gruesome detail, the same claustrophobic atmosphere, the same sense of human beings being relentlessly stripped of their humanity. But the focus of the two films is very different. In *Cool Hand Luke* the authorities are stereotyped; in *Brubaker* the prisoners and politicians verge on such indeterminacy. In place of Newman's animalistic prisoner we have Redford's cerebral governor. Yet Luke is a complex character, which can hardly be said of Brubaker; he is a goodie, and the principal forces ranged against him, both within and without the prison, are corrupt to the bone. As a result the most interesting sequences in *Brubaker* are those involving the two ambivalent characters, the liberal establishment figure Lillian Grey and the cynical but decent trustee Dickie Coombes (Yaphet Kotto).

It was another part Redford didn't particularly want from an acting point of view. The character was 'anchored in the centre of all this action going on ... the tendency is you can either be viewed as too stolid or too heroic or too passive or whatever. That's just the risk you run.' *Brubaker* was 'something I felt was important'. And since 'it looked like it wouldn't get made with an unknown ... committing to it might help the picture get made.'

Prison reform is indeed an important subject, but presumably much of Redford's interest in *Brubaker* lay in its treatment of the theme which he was making his own—the exploration of what space was available for the principled individual, and the effectiveness of such an individual in the matter of moving social mountains. Henry Brubaker makes all this available

Previous page: *A lack of trust. With Yaphet Kotto*
Opposite: *Digging for truth*
Both from Brubaker *(1979)*

space his own; his unwillingness to surrender any of it dominates the film. It is this refusal to compromise which wins him the eventual respect of the rankmen, and which also ensures his eventual dismissal. The prison board and the trustees have been waiting in vain for Brubaker to realise that the space must be shared, but he knows that such a compromise would constitute a victory for them; it would leave everything essentially unchanged. His refusal to bend might get him dismissed—also a victory for them—but it also gives him his only chance to break the pattern, and so make change a real possibility.

Caught between these warring factions, the two ambivalent characters do their best to slow Brubaker down. Lillian Grey fears that he will throw away all his gains by pushing too fast and too hard; she tells him straight, 'if you're not in the system, you can't change it'. Dickie Coombes fears that too many innocents will die in a crusade which is bound to fail. When the old prisoner is tortured and killed for revealing the location of the mass graveyard, Coombes bitterly blames Brubaker, and the latter is reduced to muttering 'perhaps you're right'. But this is his only moment of weakness; the basic thrust of the film 'proves' both Grey and Coombes wrong. In the long run it is Brubaker's child-like determination to brook no obstacles, to defend every last inch of his principles, which proves the successful strategy.

Previous page: *The reformers. With Jane Alexander*
Opposite: *Brubaker reveals that he is the new warden*
Both from Brubaker

Henry Brubaker is a curious hybrid character. Neither insider nor outsider, he exists physically within the system yet mentally outside it. He has absorbed the two lessons of the sixties, that a corrupt establishment cannot be bargained with, and that frontal assault cannot be successful. But rather than *conclude* from this that it's all hopeless, he *begins* by assuming as much. In a sense this Redford persona is the frontier American reborn, concerned not with mending or extending civilisation but with creating it. Modern America is the new wilderness, and the Brubakers who stalk through its undergrowth are preachers and tamers, men who can no more compromise with state prison boards than their forbears could compromise with mountain lions. Bernsteins and Woodwards can unseat Presidents, but there will always be more waiting in line, less corrupt perhaps, but still trapped within a systemic web of corruption. The Brubakers know where the real enemy lies, and the Sonny Steeles know that you can't hope to deal with it on its own poisoned ground. As Brubaker says: 'before any real change can occur, we have to begin to tell ourselves the whole truth'.

Previous page: *Inside information. With David Keith and Jon Van Ness*
Opposite: *Prison-fare*
Both from Brubaker

Ordinary people?

After completing work on *All The President's Men* in 1976, Redford had decided on a two-year 'leave of absence' from the acting profession. He wanted to get things in perspective again, think about his future, about where he was going. This 'leave', though interrupted by *A Bridge Too Far* and curtailed by *The Electric Horseman*, seems to have been productive. At last the long-delayed move into directing was taking shape.

There were several reasons for this shift. His attitude towards acting had always been ambivalent, and the more success he enjoyed as an actor-star the more Redford's ambivalence seemed to grow. He was being offered a steady stream of juicy, money-spinning roles—like the lead in the film version of the best-selling *The Thorn Birds* and the Rhett Butler role in the planned *Gone With The Wind* sequel but he could not work up any enthusiasm for them. 'I kept telling people, "I don't want to be son of Gable." I never aimed to be a sex symbol, a classical actor, a box-office draw or any of those things. I just did my job, went home and rereated, and put myself as far away from the movie star thing as I could.'

Acting seemed less and less relevant to his real concerns, and his early, adolescent distaste for it as a profession emerged once more. 'Now I realise,' he was to say in 1981, 'I never really cared for acting. I used to think it was girlish when I was a kid, and probably I got into it because I was fairly lazy, or I had no other plans, and I enjoyed the attention up to a point. Everyone likes taking centre-stage, but few individuals like the heavy price of fame,

and of that silly adulation of fans who simply cherish you because you've one particular hair colour and have one or another certain set of eyes and nose and mouth. I mean, it's so meaningless.'

But this distaste for the life of the actor-star did not extend to cover all work in the cinema industry. Indeed, as regards *All The President's Men*, *The Electric Horseman* and *Brubaker*, Redford had been very much involved in the total creative process, offering inputs all along the line from conception to distribution. It was only the acting part which seemed to offer so few challenges and to cost so much in personal terms. It was the actor who was turned into a dehumanised symbol; it was the director who got most of the creative satisfaction.

Redford had been thinking about directing for years, and yet shying away from taking the decisive plunge. 'Directing used to frighten me, but it also fascinated me. It took me a long time to do it, because I must have known, in the back of my younger mind, that it would be a lifelong commitment.' It was a serious business, an artistic business, carrying a sense of vocation which Redford had felt for painting, but never for acting. Recovering this sense of vocation was to be immensely satisfying. 'I thought I'd lost my career in art or my way in art,' he later said. 'I thought I would never see that again in my life. And that was sad. It would be reduced to being like a hobby. The pleasure in finding that I could bring it back and incorporate it into

Opposite: *Redford in thoughtful mood*
Following: *Directing Mary Tyler Moore in* Ordinary People *(1980)*

196

another field I had developed in was really exciting.'

He would be in control at last. Of course his status, not to mention his intelligence, had given him a great influence over many of his films as an actor, but influence was not control. As director he would now have the final say; the movie would ultimately be *his*. 'When I direct, I can really say I've *done* a film. I've made a major input into it and I've created *and* completed a vision that takes in all the characters, the story and many more aspects.'

There was one obvious difficulty to be overcome. The sort of films he wanted to make did not seem to be the sort that the industry wanted made or the public wanted to see. Redford was not interested in material involving car chases, space battles, the pornographication of sex or violence; he wanted to make films about 'behaviour and feeling', hardly the stuff of which moguls' dreams are made.

Of course, Redford had not been much interested in such dreams as an actor, and was certainly uninterested in launching his directorial career with anything that smacked of compromise. When, in the summer of 1976, he read the galley proofs of Judith Guest's novel *Ordinary People*, and found that it admirably suited *his* requirements, he bought the screen rights. Commercial or not, it deserved to be filmed. At this point it had not been decided who was to direct, but as Redford's resolve to move behind the camera hardened, and as the book burgeoned into a bestseller, it became obvious that this would be the chosen vehicle for his own debut. He could both do what he wanted to do and keep the moguls smiling. It was an auspicious mix of circumstances, owing something to luck and something more to Redford's determi-

nation and insight.

Ordinary People is about the Jarrett family's inability to cope. Their material circumstances are far from inadequate, but the death of older son Buck in a boating accident has opened up a can of psychological worms, driving younger son Conrad (Timothy Hutton) to attempt suicide, mother Beth (Mary Tyler Moore) further into an already over-protected self, and father Calvin (Donald Sutherland) to ineffectually agonise over what the hell's gone wrong with his family. The parents send Conrad to a psychiatrist (Judd Hirsch), but Beth's adamant refusal to recognise that the problems extend beyond Conrad's psyche precludes any solution to the wider family crisis. Conrad is 'cured', but only after 'his' problems have driven a stake through the heart of his parents' marriage.

There is a great deal wrong with *Ordinary People*, more that is right with it, and much that is of interest to any analysis of Redford's film career. The principal objection can be simply put—for a story which rests so heavily on individuals and individuality, the leading characters are over-stereotyped. Beth is too invulnerable, Calvin too ineffectual, the psychiatrist too understanding and too effective. Each seems more like a vehicle for a particular state of mind than a real person, and this despite acting performances of undisputed quality. Only Conrad is allowed a full range of expression, and his 'cure' is just too good an advert for the therapist's

Opposite: *Dressed for an Oscar?*
Following page: *Directing Timothy Hutton in Ordinary People*

couch.

The title of the film, as Redford admitted, is 'something of a misnomer'. The inhabitants of affluent Lake Forest are hardly ordinary in a socio-economic sense, but this fact is of limited importance. The life they lead—the possessions, the ease, the clean-cut kids and the golf—is exactly that life which millions of less fortunate Americans aspire to. It is the version of middle-class paradise which has been idealised in American television sitcoms (including *The Mary Tyler Moore Show*) for decades. It is by now an ordinary dream. What never comes across in the film is the extent to which the very realisation of that dream has made it more difficult for the dreamers to face reality.

More serious, from the film's point of view, is its dramatic reliance on the one thing which makes the Jarretts extraordinary—the death of older son Buck. If Redford was trying to say something about middle-class America, about 'that part of America which really makes it go' as he put it, then the particularity of the Jarretts' situation was bound to weaken the universal applicability of the statement intended.

Two related objections are the over-concentration on the one family and the general obsession (exemplified by the psycho-therapeutic theme) with individual motivation as the prime causal factor at work in family, and by implication social, history. This is not to suggest that every movie needs an upfront class analysis, or that shots of burning Miami should have been eye-catchingly showing on television as the family falls to pieces, but it does seem that *Ordinary People* would have greatly benefitted from being opened out more. Almost all the best scenes involve the family in contact with the 'outside world'. Conrad's conversations with his swimming instructor, for example, besides being heavily redolent of earlier Redford themes, tell us more about America than the Jarretts together tell us throughout the movie. Conrad and his new girlfriend, the parents at the party, the family at the grandparents'—all these sequences are brilliantly accomplished, and highly expressive of the family's problems. But when the three principals are inter-relating on the screen there is only the clipped conversations, the suggestive glances, all telling us what we already know—they're screwed up—without moving us any further into why. Their problem becomes the film's problem.

Redford's weakness as an actor, his tendency towards over-understatement, may prove his weakness as a director. He seems too restrained, too reliant on suggestion and not enough on explanation. This is most true in *Ordinary People* of Beth, the central character in many ways, who is supposed to seem both weak and strong. Unfortunately the overwhelming impression is one of a stone wall. Of course we are invited to guess the reasons for her being this way, and we are shown the symptoms of the disease, but we are never taken into the question of how or why she, or anyone else, gets this way. What should have been a central purpose of the film becomes just a given fact.

On the other side of the fence, the slickness of Conrad's recovery is ad-

With Lola at the Oscar ceremony

204

equately balanced by the parents' failure to resolve their situation. There is no crassly happy ending. The general understated tone, by letting few bells ring, at least ensures that none ring out of tune. And it is certainly true that Redford's restraint as an actor was a strength as well as a weakness. *Ordinary People* suggests that the same will be true of his directing. The unwillingness to over-dramatise, to let the characters 'speak' for themselves, is what gives the film its hard edge, its semi-documentary feel, its authenticity. This is particularly noteworthy in that such subject-matter, in the hands of a director more inclined to dramatise, could well have slid the film down a more slippery slope, into the dreaded mire of soap opera.

All these are major plusses. But what is most encouraging about *Ordinary People* is the subject-matter itself. If someone is willing to make films about people rather than about events, to deal in emotional violence rather than blood, in compassion rather than greed, then he or she should be roundly applauded. In particular the American middle classes have, as Redford says, been over-neglected by the cinema industry. The very rich and the desperate poor are perhaps easier to dramatise, but no sector of the population is more crucial to the society's future than this middle-class world of realised dreams and unexpected nightmares. This is Reagan's constituency. This is where the rot sets in. As Yeats once noted in a moment of inspiration, things tend to fall apart when the centre fails to hold.

On his way to an Oscar?

Goodbye and hello

Few directors have enjoyed such auspicious debuts. *Ordinary People* proved a commercial success, a qualified critical success, and an Oscar-winner. If Redford had harboured any doubts as to his ability to make the transition, then they must by now be much diminished. He will not lack for financial backing in future ventures. He can look forward, with confident relish, to the new challenges involved in the unfolding of his new career.

As for the old challenges which faced the actor, they now seem like mere preparation, necessary stepping-stones on the path to the canvas chair. His days as an actor, he says, 'are numbered. I'm into middle age, and I'm more mature in many ways. I'm too mature, mentally and soon physically, to continue being any kind of sex symbol. My kids are grown up now, and I care what they think; before, they were children, and it didn't matter that their father wore make-up and cavorted on the screen with actresses in designer outfits, but now I have a need for more personal commitment and personal dignity. The world has grown up fast, it's become a very serious place, and I think I want to spend my time more wisely.

'I'm still talking with a couple of studios about things I'm committed to as an actor, but I am retiring from films, definitely. Not right away, but semi-gradually; by or before the mid-1980s I won't be an actor anymore. My next project, I'm fairly sure, will be as a director, and then one or two movies as an actor, and that should do it.'

One of those two movies is likely to re-team Redford and Streisand for a sequel to *The Way We Were*. The other remains undecided, perhaps the long-delayed *A Place To Come To* or the unmade Western *Mayberley's Kill*. Either way the Redford-as-actor canon, now comprising twenty-two films, seems near completion.

His acting style has almost invariably seemed effortless. If the test of a good actor is that he or she doesn't seem to be acting, then Redford has long since graduated. He has nearly always been convincing, even when called upon to play characters, like Big Halsy or Bob Woodward, which cut right across the grain of his image. His good looks have naturally helped him to stardom, but they have sometimes proved a hindrance to the actor, and it is at such times that his ability has been most marked.

His choice of projects has been somewhat inconsistent, and the range of directors with whom he has worked has been unusually narrow. This latter may prove a limitation on his directorial talents, but it has not particularly hampered his work as an actor. His most fruitful work has arisen from the collaborations with Sydney Pollack (*This Property is Condemned, Jeremiah Johnson, The Way We Were, Three Days of the Condor, The Electric Horseman*) and Michael Ritchie (*Downhill Racer, The Candidate*), but there have also been successful one-off encounters with Arthur Penn (*The Chase*), Abraham Polonsky (*Tell Them Willie Boy Is Here*), Alan Pakula (*All The President's Men*) and Stuart Rosenberg (*Brubaker*). These eleven films represent the cream of Redford's cinematic milk-bottle, and any bottle of milk which is half-full of cream represents a considerable achievement. Taken together these eleven films represent a decade spent, consciously or unsconsciously, in exploring the emotional and political contours of American life. None of these films has sacrificed a thoughtful approach to the needs of commerciality, yet many of them have proved commercial successes. If in some cases the balance betwen accessibility and depth has not been quite right, then that is to be expected. If mainstream commercial cinema was a naturally thoughtful medium, then a lot of star actors and directors would be elsewhere employed.

It is obviously too early to reach any firm conclusions as to Redford's talent in the directorial chair. *Ordinary People*, though spectacularly successful on Hollywood's terms, represents little more than a sound platform for future endeavour in artistic terms. Much will depend on Redford's ability to pick out the right material, and here the signs are encouraging— nearly all of his best films as an actor were films to which he was personally and artistically committed. His instincts seem better than sound.

It is not the purpose of this book to pass any judgements on Redford the man, except insofar as the personality affects the work. He is clearly a complex and, in some ways, confused person, for only such a person could have mirrored so satisfactorily the confusingly complex issues which face the developed West in the final quarter of this century. His attitudes, as expressed to the media, seem highly ambivalent, as befits a conservative rebel. If his much-publicised belief in marital loyalty seems a throwback to the past, and suspiciously chauvinist in content, it also seems a welcome relief from the soulless and irresponsible libertarianism of the sixties. If his devotion to ecological matters could sometimes be construed as an avoidance of the real political issues facing America, at other times it could equally well be con-

209

strued as embracing them. Redford may prove unable to find a balance between such conflicting causes which pleases everyone, but in that he will not be alone. What is important is that he still seems to be trying, still seems to be growing. And that, for a Hollywood star, is no mean feat.

His lifestyle and politics have been the subject of some bitter attacks. Thus Alexander Walker in his book *Double Takes*: 'What Redford does not like to emphasise, if indeed he is aware of it, is that his way of conserving nature is actually an oasis for the favoured few; that his concern with reclaiming land is one way of keeping unwelcome folk from fouling his doorstep; that all the diurnal activities at Sundance, improving the soil, raising scholarships for Indians, re-stocking the trout streams, abating noise, planting forests—are actually the luxury mutation of a pioneering community. If one asks whose quality of life is improved, the answer must be "the owners".'

This is doubtless true, but is it to the point? What could Redford do to answer such criticism? Corrupt the soil, forget the Indians and de-stock the trout streams? Move? Should he join the glittering parade in Beverley Hills, drinking and hyping by day, drinking and spouse-swapping by night? No man is an island, as somebody once pointed out, and Redford's 'luxury mutation' is at least a positive step for someone. As a source of envy or a model of emulation it seems infinitely preferable to the endless clash of empty heads and over-full stomachs currently on display in the Hollywood ghetto.

Of course, Redford must not base his film-work on the political premise that everyone has the option to live the way he does. Not everyone can escape the society he detests, and fewer still can afford to purchase a mountain. In his films he can show us the clean winds and clouds, but he must also dig a little into the urban dirt if he wishes to be regarded as an American artist of perception and stature. He must confront the reality of his nation. Part of it can be seen from his porch in the Wasatch Mountains, another part was on show in the story of the Lake Forest Jarretts. But there is much more to explore, a whole new wilderness for a directorial Brubaker to tame.

There are reasons for hope. Already the failures of Sheriff Cooper and Hubbell Gardiner have been consigned to oblivion by the principled stands of Sonny Steele and Henry Brubaker. Perhaps one day Jeremiah Johnson will find a better way to express his heroism than through the slaughter of another race. America has to come of age, and Robert Redford is one of the many Americans who have it in their power to help it along the way.

The winning smile?

It was all worth it. Redford receives his oscar as Best Director for Ordinary People

Filmography

War Hunt (1962)
Director: Denis Sanders. Screenplay: Stanford Whitmore. Producer: Terry Sanders. Co-star: John Saxon. Character: Pvt Roy Loomis.

Situation Hopeless—But Not Serious (1965)
Director: Gottfried Reinhardt. Screenplay: Silvia Reinhardt, from Robert Shaw's novel *The Hiding Place*. Producer: Gottfried Reinhardt. Co-stars: Alec Guinness, Michael Connors. Character: Hank.

Inside Daisy Clover (1965)
Director: Robert Mulligan. Screenplay: Gavin Lambert, from his own novel. Producer: Alan J. Pakula. Co-stars: Natalie Wood, Christopher Plummer, Roddy McDowall. Character: Wade Lewis.

The Chase (1966)
Director: Arthur Penn. Screenplay: Lillian Hellman, from Horton Foote's play and novel. Producer: Sam Spiegel. Co-stars: Marlon Brando, Jane Fonda, E. G. Marshall, James Fox, Angie Dickinson, Janice Rule, Robert Duvall. Character: Bubber Reeves.

This Property is Condemned (1966)
Director: Sydney Pollack. Screenplay: Francis Ford Coppola, Fred Coe and Edith Sommer, suggested by Tennessee Williams, one-act play. Producer: John Houseman. Co-stars: Natalie Wood, Kate Reid, Charles Bronson. Character: Owen Legate.

Barefoot in the Park (1967)
Director: Gene Saks. Screenplay: Neil Simon, from his own play. Producer: Hal Wallis. Co-stars: Jane Fonda, Mildred Natwick, Charles Boyer. Character: Paul Bratter.

Butch Cassidy and the Sundance Kid (1969)
Director: George Roy Hill. Screenplay: William Goldman. Producer: John Foreman. Executive Producer: Paul Monash. Co-stars: Paul Newman, Katherine Ross. Character: The Sundance Kid.

The Downhill Racer (1969) (UK—**Downhill Racer**)
Director: Michael Ritchie. Screenplay: James Salter. Producer: Richard Gregson. Co-stars: Gene Hackman, Camilla Sparv. Character: David Chappellet.

Tell Them Willie Boy Is Here (1969)
Director: Abraham Polonsky. Screenplay: Abraham Polonsky, from Harry Lawton's novel *Willie Boy*. Producer: Philip A. Waxman. Co-stars: Robert Blake, Katherine Ross, Susan Clark. Character: Sheriff Cooper.

Little Fauss and Big Halsy (1970)
Director: Sidney J. Furie. Screenplay: Charles Eastman. Producer: Albert J. Ruddy. Co-stars: Michael J. Pollard, Lauren Hutton. Character: Big Halsy.

The Hot Rock (1972) (UK—**How to Steal a Diamond in Four Uneasy Lessons**)
Director: Peter Yates. Screenplay: William Goldman, from Donald E. Westlake's novel. Producers: Hal Lander and Bobby Roberts. Co-stars: George Segal, Ron Leibman, Paul Sand, Zero Mostel. Character: Dortmunder.

The Candidate (1972)
Director: Michael Ritchie. Screenplay: Jeremy Larner. Producer: Walter Coblenz. Co-stars: Peter Boyle, Don Porter, Karen Carlson. Character: Bill McKay.

Jeremiah Johnson (1972)
Director: Sydney Pollack. Screenplay: John Milius and Edward Anhalt, from *Mountain Man* by Vardis Fisher and *Crow Killer* by Raymond W. Thorp and Robert Bunker. Producer: Joe Wizan. Co-stars: Will Geer, Stephan Gierasch, Allyn Ann McLerie, Charles Tyner, Delle Bolton, Josh Albee. Character: Jeremiah Johnson.

The Way We Were (1973)
Director: Sydney Pollack. Screenplay: Arthur Laurents, from his own novel. Producer: Ray Stark. Co-stars: Barbra Streisand, Bradford Dillman, Lois Chiles, Patrick O'Neal, Viveca Lindfors. Character: Hubbell Gardiner.

The Sting (1973)
Director: George Roy Hill. Screenplay: David S. Ward. Producers: Tony Bill, Michael Phillips, Julia Phillips. Co-stars: Paul Newman, Robert Shaw. Character: Johnny Hooker.

The Great Gatsby (1974)
Director: Jack Clayton. Screenplay: Francis Ford Coppola, from F. Scott Fitzgerald's novel. Producer: David Merrick. Co-stars: Mia Farrow, Sam Waterston, Bruce Dern, Karen Black, Scott Wilson, Lois Chiles. Character: Jay Gatsby.

The Great Waldo Pepper (1975)
Director: George Roy Hill. Screenplay: William Goldman, from a story by George Roy Hill. Producer: George Roy Hill. Co-stars: Bo Svenson, Susan Sarandon, Margot Kidder, Edward Herrmann, Bo Brundin. Character: Waldo Pepper.

Three Days of the Condor (1975)
Director: Sydney Pollack. Screenplay: Lorenzo Semple Jr. and David Rayfiel, from James Grady's novel *Six Days of the Condor*. Producer: Stanley Schneider. Co-stars: Faye Dunaway, Max Von Sydow, Cliff Robertson. Character: Joseph Turner.

All The President's Men (1976)
Director: Alan J. Pakula. Screenplay: William Goldman, from book by Carl Bernstein and Bob Woodward. Producer: Walter Coblenz. Co-stars: Dustin Hoffman, Jack Warden, Martin Balsam, Hal Holbrook, Jason Robards, Jane Alexander. Character: Bob Woodward.

A Bridge Too Far (1977)
Director: Richard Attenborough. Screenplay: William Goldman, from Cornelius Ryan's book. Producers: Joseph E. Levine, Richard P. Levine. Co-stars: Dirk Bogarde, James Caan, Michael Caine, Sean Connery, Elliot Gould, Gene Hackman, Anthony Hopkins, Hardy Kruger, Laurence Olivier, Ryan O'Neal, Maximilian Schell, Liv Ullman. Character: Major Julian Cook.

The Electric Horseman (1978)
Director: Sydney Pollack. Screenplay: Robert Garland. Producer: Ray Stark. Co-stars: Jane Fonda, Willie Nelson, Valerie Perrine. Character: Sonny Steele.

Brubaker (1979)
Director: Stuart Rosenberg. Screenplay: W. D. Richter. Producer: Ron Silverman. Co-stars: Yaphet Kotto, Jane Alexander, Murray Hamilton, David Keith, Tim McIntire. Character: Henry Brubaker.

Ordinary People (1980)
Director: Robert Redford. Screenplay: Alvin Sargent. Producer: Ronald L. Schwary. Stars: Mary Tyler Moore, Donald Sutherland, Timothy Hutton, Judd Hirsch.

Index